Fiction Attack!

Insider Secrets for Writing and Selling Your Novels & Stories
For Self-Published and Traditional Authors

James Scott Bell

Compendium Press

ISBN: 978-0-910355-08-7

Compendium Press
P.O. Box 705
Woodland Hills, CA 91365

Also by James Scott Bell

On Writing:

Plot & Structure
Revision & Self-Editing for Publication
The Art of War for Writers
Conflict & Suspense

Fiction:

One More Lie
Watch Your Back
Deceived
Try Dying
Try Darkness
Try Fear
Pay Me in Flesh (as K. Bennett)
The Year of Eating Dangerously (as K. Bennett)
I Ate the Sheriff (as K. Bennett)
City of Angels
Angels Flight
Angel of Mercy
A Greater Glory
A Higher Justice
A Certain Truth
Glimpses of Paradise
No Legal Grounds
The Whole Truth
Presumed Guilty
Sins of the Fathers
Breach of Promise
Deadlock
The Nephilim Seed
Blind Justice
Final Witness
Circumstantial Evidence
The Darwin Conspiracy

Also by James Scott Bell

On Writing:

Plot & Structure
Revision & Self-Editing for Publication
The Art of War for Writers
Conflict & Suspense

Fiction:

One More Lie
Watch Your Back
Deceived
Try Dying
Try Darkness
Try Fear
Pay Me in Flesh (as K. Bennett)
The Year of Eating Dangerously (as K. Bennett)
I Ate the Sheriff (as K. Bennett)
City of Angels
Angels Flight
Angel of Mercy
A Greater Glory
A Higher Justice
A Certain Truth
Glimpses of Paradise
No Legal Grounds
The Whole Truth
Presumed Guilty
Sins of the Fathers
Breach of Promise
Deadlock
The Nephilim Seed
Blind Justice
Final Witness
Circumstantial Evidence
The Darwin Conspiracy

Table of Contents

Life Pitched High

Can you identify the moment in your life when you made the decision *I am going to be a writer?*

What did it feel like? What does it feel like now?

Perhaps the best novel about a writer, Jack London's semi-autobiographical *Martin Eden*, captures these singular passions in a memorable way. Early in the novel young Martin is at sea, returning to San Francisco, when the idea takes hold:

And then, in splendor and glory, came the great idea. He would write. He would be one of the eyes through which the world saw, one of the ears through which it heard, one of the hearts through which it felt. He would write — everything — poetry and prose, fiction and description, and plays like Shakespeare. There was career and the way to win to Ruth. The men of literature were the world's giants

. . . Once the idea had germinated, it mastered him, and the return voyage to San Francisco was like a dream. He was drunken with unguessed power and felt that he could do anything . . . To write! The thought was fire in him. He would begin as soon as he got back . . . There were twenty-four hours in each day. He was invincible. He knew how to work, and the citadels would go down before him.

Back on land, Martin sets out with zeal, up to 18 hours a day of it, to realize his writing dream:

He was profoundly happy. Life was pitched high. He was in a fever that never broke. The joy of creation that is supposed to belong to the gods was his. All the life about him—the odors of stale vegetables and soapsuds, the slatternly form of his sister, and the jeering face of Mr. Higginbotham—was a dream. The real world was in his mind, and the stories he wrote were so many pieces of reality out of his mind.

I can pinpoint the day I took the big dive into writing. It was in 1988 and I went with my wife to see a double feature. The movie I really wanted to see was *Wall Street.* The movie it was playing with I didn't know that much about, except that it starred Cher.

That movie was *Moonstruck,* and it knocked me out.

I was a practicing lawyer at the time and had been told writers were born, not made. I had believed that for ten years.

But *Moonstruck* was so good I knew I had to try to learn to write, even if I failed. I was determined to use the study disciplines I'd picked up in law school to find out how to write fiction. In my journal I wrote: *Today I have decided to become a writer.*

And I was soon lost in the joy of creating, like Martin Eden. I still remember those early years of writing and discovering as primarily joyous.

And you know what? All these years later, having published almost 40 books, I still find learning about the craft of fiction *exciting.* Even if I read about a technique I know, but get a slightly different take on it from the author, I feel a surge of happiness. Because I love what I do and I love anything that helps me get better.

I also love helping other writers. I've been doing it for almost twenty years now, and when I see light bulbs go off in a student's eyes, I'm just as jazzed as I am when I myself learn something new.

So that's why I am offering this book to you now. It's full of the best stuff I know about writing and the writing life. Much of it is a collection of posts on writing I've done for The Kill Zone blog, but grouped in categories for your convenience. It is a companion to my other collection, *Writing Fiction for All You're Worth.*

I do hope you enjoy it, and find a little of that Jack London fire inside you.

Keep writing.
James Scott Bell

The Writing Craft

My Aha! Moment

Some time ago I got a lovely email that begins:

> I want to send you a big, sincere "thank you" for
> writing your book on plot and structure.
>
> After trawling through many books on plotting and
> feeling more and more confused and anxious it was
> a relief to come across your book. Finally I began
> having "'aha!" moments — and I've only read three
> chapters!
>
> You are so encouraging and the exercises are really
> useful — although now I find myself watching
> television and asking "what if?" a great deal of the
> time . . .

If an ex-lawyer can still have working cockles in his heart, mine were warmed. I love hearing when a writer starts to get it. An "aha moment" is exactly what I strive to provide in my writing books and workshops. Because it was just such a moment that put me on the path to selling my work.

I know exactly when it was, too, because I've kept a diary of my writing life. On September 15, 1990, I wrote these words:

> EPIPHANY!
>
> Light! A bulb! A flash! A revelation! My muse on fire!
>
> I feel like I've suddenly "clicked into" how to write . . . I mean, everything I've been reading and brooding about for the last year has finally locked. There is this tremendous rush of exhilaration. It just happened, and now I feel like everything I write will be at least GOOD, but can also be EXCELLENT.

I was writing screenplays at the time, and I'd written five or six over two years without success. But the next one I wrote was optioned and got me into a top agency. I optioned other properties, too, but when they didn't get pushed up the ladder (an old Hollywood story) I got frustrated and wrote a novel, using the same revealed wisdom. The novel sold and came out in 1995. Then I wrote a legal thriller and got a five-book contract. I've not been without a contract since.

And all of it I trace back to that epiphany. Here's the story.

I was a member of the Writer's Digest Book Club at the time. One of their offerings was by Jack Bickham, *Writing Novels That Sell.* I'd been reading screenplay books, like Syd Field's *Screenplay* and Linda Seger's *Making a Good Script Great.* I thought, well, there may be some cross-over here from the novel world, and I bought the book.

Bickham advised this was a book for people wanting to get serious about becoming professional writers. Not fluff, only what had worked for him and his writing students at the University of Oklahoma. He said it should be studied sequentially, as each chapter built upon the last.

So that's what I did, starting at page one and working my way through. And when I got to Chapter 8, covering "scene and sequel," that's when the bulbs started popping in my brain.

Up to that time I did not have a strategic approach to writing the next scene. I just sort of let it bubble up in my imagination (or had committed to it on an index card) and went for it. But my scripts weren't working. People told me this, but couldn't tell me why, which was frustrating beyond measure.

Now, suddenly, I *knew* why they weren't working. A superb writing instructor had nailed it and explained it to me.

In brief, a scene is a unit of action made up of a goal, conflict and disaster. The disaster doesn't always mean something huge, though it sometimes is. It is a setback of some sort, making the hero's situation worse.

I have the key paragraph highlighted in yellow, and underlined in red, in Bickham's book:

> We make our story go forward by pushing our hero backward, farther and farther from his ultimate goal, through scene disasters. The reader reads excitedly, roots for the hero--then is crushed with him. The novel flies along, lifelike, dramatic, suspenseful, hard to put down, filled with twists, surprises and setbacks--and more and more tension as well as admiration for the battered hero who simply won't quit.

Bam. Boom. Bingo. This was my breakthrough, my foundation. And it's never let me down since.

I have had many lesser "aha moments" since then. I keep studying the craft, because it keeps me fresh. It sometimes gives me new insights. I hope that as you read this, you'll have your own moments of realization. I'm here to help.

How Not to Write Your Novel

There are a lot of ways not to do something.

Like the new boat owner a few years ago who was filling up his pleasure craft with fuel for that first time out. Only he mistook the tube that is meant to hold fishing poles for the gas tank. After completing his work he started up the engine.

The gas fumes ignited and blew the boat owner into the sky. He came down in the drink and was rescued, but the boat was a goner.

You can be just as creative in finding ways *not* to write your novel. With a little thought and not much effort, you can easily devise methods to prevent you from actually finishing your book. Or finishing a book that has a chance to sell.

So if not finishing or not selling are your goals, I'm here to help you with the following tips:

Wait for Inspiration

Go to your favorite writing spot with your laptop or pad. Perhaps it's a Starbucks, maybe a library, or it could be your own kitchen table. Sit down with a cup of coffee and hold it in two hands. Sip it slowly. Do not put your fingers anywhere near the keyboard.

Glance outside a window if one is available. Wait for a skein of geese flying in V formation.

If you're in public and no window is available, simply observe the other patrons and make sure they can see your expression of other-worldly concentration.

You are waiting for inspiration. It must come to from on high and fill you like fire.

Until then, do not write a word. If you're tempted to start working, open up Spider Solitaire immediately. Tell yourself this will relax the mind so inspiration can pour in.

If you must, type a few sentences, but then sit back and tell yourself they're not good enough, and repeat the above pattern.

If you spend three or four hours in this fashion, it will be time well spent in not writing your novel.

Of course, those who think it wise to finish their novel do things backwards. They don't wait for inspiration. They go after it, as Jack London said he did, "with a club." They follow the advice of Peter DeVries, who said, "I only write when I'm inspired, and I make sure I'm inspired every morning at 9 a.m."

These poor souls think the secret to writing a novel is to write, and work through minor problems quickly and major ones after the first draft is done.

They do things like this:

Establish a writing quota. A quota based not on how much time they spend thinking about writing, but how many words they get down. Some do a daily quota, others do it by the week. But they figure out what they can comfortably get done and set a quota about 10% above that as a goal to shoot for.

Review the previous day's writing and then move on. By looking at what they wrote the day before, they get back into the flow of their story. They fix little things, spelling and style mostly, but then get on with the day's current work.

And then they look up one day and see a finished manuscript. They have lost sight of how not to write a novel.

Look Over Your Shoulder

It was a great pitcher Satchel Paige who said, "Don't look back, something may be gaining on you."

It's good life advice, but in order to *not* write your novel, you must ignore it.

To not write your novel, constantly worry about how bad your book might turn out to be. Pause every thousand words or so and think, *This is about the worst piece of crud known to man. Where did I put the bourbon?*

This is sometimes known as the "inner critic," and he is your best friend for not writing a novel.

If you think about those doubts long enough, you can even develop them into fears. Jack Bickham, a novelist who was even better known for his books on the craft, put it this way:

> All of us are scared: of looking dumb, of running out of ideas, of never selling our copy, of not getting noticed. We fiction writers make a business of being scared, and not just of looking dumb. Some of these fears may never

go away, and we may just have to learn to live with them.

Of course, some writers learn not only to live with doubt and fear, but defeat them. How do they do that? Mostly they simply pound away at the keyboard.

They concentrate on the words in front of them and kick that inner critic to the curb.

They train themselves to do this via writing exercises, such as:

The Five Minute Non-Stop. Write for five minutes, first thing in the morning if possible, without stopping to think about what you're writing. No correcting. Just write.

The Page Long Sentence. Choose something to describe (a room or a character) and write a page-long sentence about it, not pausing to edit and going on whatever tangents present themselves.

The List Maker. Whenever you're stuck for an idea to pursue, make a list. Brainstorm ideas without assessing them. Get lots of ideas, then pick the best one.

Writers who have dulled the inner critic don't worry about getting the words right. They get the words *written*.

They really have not got this not writing a novel thing down at all.

Ignore the Craft

This piece of advice on how not to write a novel applies whether you finish your first draft or not. It is the cry of the artistic rebel who will go to the grave denouncing rules and techniques and anything that gets within a hundred yards of structure.

This does create a very good feeling, like you are the king of the world. You can completely ignore all the storytellers who came before you (be sure to call them hacks or sell-outs). The fact that you will mostly likely not place your book anywhere, or even get many digital download readers to care, should not hinder you from your intractable course.

The misdirected scribes who actually sell their books and build readerships take the craft of writing seriously. They study it without apology. They have people give them feedback—editors, critique groups, trusted and objective friends—and they read countless novels and analyze what's going on. They'll ask questions such as:

- How does the writer make me want to turn the page?
- Why am I drawn to the Lead character?
- When are the stakes raised?
- How does the writer integrate minor characters?
- What makes a scene work?
- What's the key to conflict?
- How does the writer handle dialogue?

These studious writers will be spotted reading *Writer's Digest* and books on writing. What they learn they apply and practice, and through the wonder of trial and error find themselves growing as writers.

But this is an article on how *not* to write a novel, so you follow their example at your peril.

Keep a Chip on Your Shoulder

Here is a surefire way not only to hold back a novel worth reading, but scuttle your career as well. Decide that arrogance and defiance are your two weapons of choice to bulldog your way to publication.

When you have a manuscript rejected, treat it as a personal insult. Think of editors and agents as being nasty creatures who love saying *No*, who sit at their computers going *Bwahahahahaha* as they fire off their favorite thing: the impersonal email or form letter.

You can carry this all to your social media sites and publicly rebuke such short-sightedness. By name.

Those who do break through to a career have the crazy idea that they can recover — even learn — from rejection and use it as motivation to write better.

They remember the admonition of writer Ron Goulart. "Never assume that a rejection of your stuff is also a rejection of you as a person. Unless it's accompanied by a punch in the nose."

Yes, they recognize that rejection hurts. Of course it does. But they know it's part of the system and always will be.

Writers like this do the following:

- They let the rejection hurt for half an hour or so, then get back to the keyboard.
- They define specifically any lesson the rejection brings.
- They understand that people in the publishing industry want to find new authors.

Of course, these are terrible tips for not writing a novel!

Write For the Market Only

Now let's talk about not writing a novel that has a chance to break through. Start by chasing the market. Write only what you think will sell. Study the bestseller lists and try to identify a trend then jump on it.

There is a saying in publishing that the moment you spot a trend it's too late to join it. By the time you finish writing something you think will be popular because it's popular now, that ship will have largely sailed.

Ignore that advice, or you may end up with something agents and editors look for: a fresh voice.

Such writers are market *conscious.* They know that publishers are in this to make money, a return on their investment in a new writer.

But they manage to bring something new to the table, namely their own heart and passion filtered through a craft that enables readers to share their vision.

Yes, vision. Any genre needs it. As super agent Donald Maas says in *The Fire in Fiction*: "What the hell are you trying to say to me?"

Writers with fresh voices:

- Concentrate on feeling the story as well as writing it.
- They revise and rewrite.
- They read outside their genre — even poetry! — to expand their stylistic range.

Let Self-Publishing be Your Short Cut

With the boom in e-books and the ease with which anything can be "published," writers have a new way *not* to write a novel that might be worth reading. It's by holding the thought firmly in mind that *whatever* they write is worth putting out as a self-published e-book, and they will do it no matter what!

This relieves a lot of the pressure of trying to grow as a writer. One can combine this with the chip-on-your-shoulder attitude for a terrific double-whammy.

Other writers, those who are laying a strong foundation in the non-traditional realm of independent publishing, continue to find ways to vet their work.

They will use test readers. The writers who are working to get better don't trust themselves in all ways. They know they need objective readers and cultivate a list of people they trust to tell them, specifically, what's not working. Then they'll figure out a way to fix that.

They will hire a good freelance editor. They know that the big plus of a traditional publisher is professional editing, so it is worth it to them to find a reputable freelance editor to go over their work (one place to check out is Writer's Digest's 2nd Draft service.) Note the word *reputable.* There are less than savory services out there that will gladly take a writer's money for very little quality work

Quit

If all else succeeds and you still are intent on not finishing your novel, or finishing one that has a chance to sell, you have a surefire fallback position: stop writing.

Forget the examples of those who persevered and eventually found an agent or got published. Like Kathryn Stockett, for example. She wrote and edited *The Help* over a five year period, then got three-and-a-half years' worth of rejections from agents––sixty in all. It was agent number sixty-one who took her on and the rest you well know.

Authors like this will tell you it's all about perseverance, the one characteristic all successful writers share. They will tell you as long as you've got a computer and keyboard, or pen and paper, you can write. And as long as you write you have a chance to get published, maybe even hit the big time.

David Eddings said, "Keep working. Keep trying. Keep believing. You still might not make it, but at least you gave it your best shot. If you don't have calluses on your soul, this isn't for you. Take up knitting instead."

I've done my job.

I've shown you how not to write a novel.

Would you rather write one instead?

Well, I'm not the writing sheriff. The choice is yours!

10 Commandments for Writers

1. Thou Shalt write a certain number of words every week

This is the first, and greatest, commandment. If you write to a quota and hold yourself to it, sooner than you think you'll have a full length novel. (I used to advocate a daily quota, but I changed it to weekly because inevitably you miss days, or life intrudes, and you can run yourself down. I also take one day off a week.) So set a weekly quota, divide it by days, and if you miss one day make it up on the others.

2. Thou Shalt write passionate first drafts

Don't edit yourself during your first drafts. The writing of it is partly an act of discovering your story, even if you outline. Write hot. Put your heart into it. Let your writer's mind run free. I edit my previous day's work and then move on. At 20,000 words I "step back" to see if I have a solid foundation, shore it up if I don't, then move on to the end. There's magic in momentum.

3. Thou Shalt make trouble for thy Lead

The engine of a good story is fueled by the threat to the Lead character. Keep turning up the heat. Make things harder. Simple three act structure: Get your Lead up a tree, throw things at him, get him down.

4. Thou Shalt put a stronger opposing force in the Lead's way

The opposition character must be stronger than the Lead. More power, more experience, more resources. Otherwise the reader won't worry. You want them to worry. Hitchcock always said the strength of his movies came from the strength and cunning of the villains. But note the opposition doesn't have to be a "bad guy." Think of Tommy Lee Jones in *The Fugitive.*

5. Thou Shalt get thy story running from the first paragraph

Start with a character, in a situation of change or threat or challenge, and grip the reader from the start. This is the opening "disturbance" and that's what readers respond to immediately. It doesn't have to be something "big." Anything that sends a ripple through the "ordinary world."

6. Thou Shalt create surprises

Avoid the predictable! Always make a list of several avenues your scenes and story might take, then choose something that makes sense but also surprises the reader.

7. Thou Shalt make everything contribute to the story

Don't go off on tangents that don't have anything to do with the characters and what they want in the story. Stay as direct as a laser beam.

(**JSB**: This one seems self-evident now, but at the time I was seeing manuscripts with scenes written for their style, not their substance. Another way to put this is the old advice to be ready to "kill your darlings.")

8. Thou Shalt cut out all the dull parts

Be ruthless in revision. Cut out anything that slows the story down. No trouble, tension or conflict is dull. At the very least, have something tense inside a character.

9. Thou Shalt develop Rhino skin

Don't take rejection or criticism personally. Learn from criticism and move on. Perseverance is the golden key to a writing career.

10. Thou Shalt never stop learning, growing and writing for the rest of thy life

Writing is growth. We learn about ourselves, we discover more about life, we use our creativity, we gain insights. At the same time, we study. Brain surgeons keep up on the journals, why should writers think they don't need to stay up on the craft? If I learn just one thing that helps me as a writer, it's worth it.

What the Hell Do You Want to Say to Me?

You have to evolve a permanent set of values to serve as motivation. — Leon Uris

At the end of his book, *The Fire in Fiction*, Donald Maass asks, "What the hell do you want to say to me?"

Which brings us to the subject of theme, or premise. It's the part of the writing craft a lot of writers seem to struggle with.

I've been reading some resources of late on the subject. Some suggest that you must know your theme up front, or your manuscript will wander. Yet many successful authors say they concentrate on the story itself and "find" the theme as they go along.

Either approach will work as long as you let the theme arise organically out of a plot that shows a character with a high stakes objective, opposed by a stronger force.

For example, in the film *The Fugitive* you have an innocent man on the run from the law, trying to find the man who murdered his wife. He's got an opposing force in the U.S. Marshals Office (embodied by Sam Gerard, super lawman). Forced to keep ahead of the law, Dr. Richard Kimble finds resources within himself he never knew existed, and eventually proves his innocence while nailing the bad guy.

So what is the theme, or premise, of *The Fugitive?* You could probably state it in a couple of ways:

– Dogged determination leads to justice
– A good man will ultimately prevail over evil
– Fighting for what's right, even against the law, leads to the truth

As a writer, you probably have a sense of what your theme is simply by knowing how your character will come out at the end. And you definitely should know at least that much.

For example, when I wrote *Try Dying* I knew my lawyer protagonist would find out who killed his fiancé, the one true love of his life, and in doing so prevail over the bad guys. In my head, then, I was thinking something along the lines of *True love will pursue justice for the slain lover, and win.*

That's what the hell I was trying to say. And I believed it passionately, which is the key to a premise that works. The reader has to believe *you* believe it.

At some point in your writing—before you begin or soon after you get going—ask the following questions:

1. At the end, what is the condition of your Lead character? Has he won or lost?

2. What is the "take away" from that condition? What will the reader think you are saying about life?

3. Most important: *Do you believe it passionately?* If not, why are you writing it?

Here's an example. In *Casablanca,* what is Rick's condition at the end of the movie? He has found a reason to stop his self-destructive behavior (drunkenness) and his isolation (because of perceived betrayal). He's found the inspiration he needs to go back into the world and rejoin the fight for freedom against the Nazis.

What's the take away? *True love will sacrifice for a greater good, and restore a person to a life worth living.*

Rick sacrifices his true love, Ilsa, because she is married to another man and that man is essential to the war effort. Rick knows that if he and Ilsa go off together she'll regret it. ("Maybe not today, maybe not tomorrow, but soon, and for the rest of your life.")

Coming as it did during the early years of World War II, it's clear the filmmakers believed this passionately, because that sort of sacrifice for a greater good is what the government was calling upon its citizens to do.

So use those three power questions to find a premise worth writing about.

Overstuffed Dialogue

A short lesson in the art of dialogue.

Here are the opening lines from an old Perry Mason show, circa 1958. A couple is in their compartment on a train:

HARRIET
I still wish I were going to Mexico with you instead of staying here in Los Angeles.

LAWRENCE
This trip's going to be too dangerous, Harriet. It's some of the most rugged terrain in the Sierra Madre mountains. It's no place for a woman, especially my wife. It's almost no place for an amateur archaeologist, either. Thanks for coming with me as far as Cole Grove station.

You see what's happening? It's an example of the writers shooting information to the viewers through expository dialogue. In fairness to the writers, that was done all the time in those old days of television.

But it's death to dialogue if you do it in your fiction.

Dialogue has to sound like it's coming from one character to another, in a way that both fits the character and the moment.

The first thing to look out for is a character saying anything that both the characters already know.

In the above example, they both know they live in Los Angeles. They both know she's his wife. They both know he's an amateur archaeologist. They both know he's going into the Sierra Madre mountains. And they both know they're going as far as Cole Grove station.

Again, we understand why it was done within the confines of a one-hour TV drama from the '50s. But you're writing a book, so don't you do it.

I was at a conference mentoring some students. One of them turned in a manuscript with the following (used by permission). A woman (Betty) has been planting bombs to avenge the death of her son. She now has a forensic investigator (Kate, who has been closing in on her) tied up, and is threatening to kill her:

Betty looked down at Kate. The triumphant smile on her face faded into a snarl at the mention of her son's death. "Why do you care?"

"Because if my son had died as a result of finding out about something terrible that had happened to him that I had kept hidden to protect him, I would want to blame the person responsible." Kate thought she would try the empathy tactic. She did feel a great sorrow for Betty and her tragic story. She watched as Betty returned her statement with a hard stare.

Here in this tense moment, Kate has revealed to Betty facts about the case, but the dialogue sounds unnatural. The long line has information stuffed into it, but it feels more like it's for the reader's benefit rather than the character's.

I told the student to go back and cut all dialogue that is not absolutely true to the character and the emotional beats. What would either of them *really* say?

Dialogue is a tool like any other in the craft. Also, dialogue is the fastest way to improve your manuscript--or sink it. If you do it well, it creates in the reader a subliminal confidence in you. They trust you as a storyteller.

If you don't do it well, confidence flies out the window.

Great dialogue keeps readers in the fictive dream. So never have a woman answer the door and say, "Oh, hello Arthur, my family doctor from Baltimore. Come in."

Compassion for Bad Guys

Unless you just got back from exploring the surface of Pluto, you are probably aware of the train wreck that was Charlie Sheen in early 2011.

It started as a bit of industry gossip. Sheen went on a radio show and started ranting about his producer in very unflattering terms. It got worse, to the point where the producer and CBS put a hold on their big hit show. Which means hundreds of millions of dollars in lost revenue. Which means this was getting serious.

The media was more than happy to put Sheen on the air, where his wild eyes and self-reflections ("I'm a total bitchin' rock star from Mars") evidenced a mind that desperately needed help. (You know things aren't going well for you when a porn actress with whom you've dallied describes you as "a sad hot mess.")

California authorities apparently agreed, and stepped in to

remove Sheen's children from his presence.

Now, I like Charlie Sheen the actor. Very talented and appealing onscreen. My three favorite Sheen films: *Wall Street, Terminal Velocity, The Arrival.*

So at first I shook my head at Sheen's unraveling, then I started to get a little ticked off at what he'd done to himself and others. Finally, sadness was added to the mix.

Yes, I know he's responsible for what drugs he put in his body, how he's treated women, and so on. He is reaping what he has sown. Still, I can't help feeling a little sorry for the guy.

Which brings me to the point of this article. When you write about train wrecks — people whose lives are a mess and who do things society generally frowns upon — you need to find your way to a compassion point. If you do, you'll write much better fiction, because the emotions you create in the reader will be more complex.

This is especially important in the writing of "bad guys." I make writing students answer this question about their villains: Why do I love this character? I force them to get deep into the background and relate to the bad guy in a tough love kind of way. As if he were a family member you deeply understand and care about. Sort of the way Martin Sheen, Charlie's dad, must feel.

The least interesting bad guys are those who are pure evil, or just crazy. The ones who stay with readers will have different levels that give off a gray, rather than a black tone.

Dean Koontz put it this way: "**The best villains are those that evoke pity and sometimes even genuine sympathy as well as terror.** Think of the pathetic aspect of the Frankenstein monster. Think of the poor werewolf, hating what he becomes in the light of the full moon, but incapable of resisting the lycanthropic tides in his own cells."

What about your bad guys? Do you love them?

Do this:

1. A deep background on your villain. Figure out his childhood, his upbringing, his schooling, his traumas.

2. Find ways to layer in that backstory into your narrative. It might be just a paragraph. It might be the subject of a flashback.

3. Find a way to give one bit of sympathy to the bad guy. Be able to see things from his perspective, even though it's wrong. Justify his behavior.

What Makes a Novel a Page Turner?

When you get right down to it, what is it that readers love most about the reading experience? I think it can be summed up quite simply. It is the emotional pleasure of being so engrossed in a story that they *must turn the page to find out what happens next.*

That means there is one thing your story absolutely *cannot* be, and that is *predictable.* To the extent that it is, reading pleasure is dissipated. This applies to any genre, of course.

So one of your goals as you begin to craft a novel is to figure out ways to pleasantly surprise the reader. For example, you avoid creating flat characters. You give us rounded characters, which E. M. Forster described as being able to surprise us in a convincing way.

Another way you create the page-turning effect is through the element of *mystery.* Not just something you find in a whodunit. No, it's well beyond that. The skillful withholding of information is one of the best things a novelist can learn to do.

Especially in the opening chapters. My rule for openings is to act first, explain later. This simple guideline will greatly increase the readability of your first pages, and even beyond. Leave mystery inherent whenever possible and explain things only progressively. Drop in hints and actions that make the reader wonder, "Why is this happening?" or "Why is she doing that? Feeling that?"

Pull the reader along with unanswered questions, saving final revelations until well into the book.

John Gilstrap does this masterfully in his novel *At All Costs.* In Chapter One, we see Jake Brighton, by all accounts a highly competent body shop manager for a Ford dealer. He's going about his business when a heavily armed team of Feds busts in and arrests him. As he's handcuffed and on the floor:

> He fought back the urge to sneeze and tried to make the pieces fit in his mind.
> *We've been so careful.*

Careful about what? Gilstrap doesn't tell us. Not until the final line of the chapter:

> He wondered if he and Carolyn still owned the tops slots on the Ten Most Wanted List.

Whoa! Another question raised: What could this outwardly normal and hardworking man have done to be at the top of the FBI list?

Again, Gilstrap makes us wait. For almost a hundred pages. As Jake and his wife Carolyn try to escape town with their thirteen-year-old son, putting a long-ago plan into effect, we are drawn further in by the mystery of their background. (In a nice twist, not even the son knows what his parents have done.)

It is only when the chase is on that Gilstrap reveals their hidden secret. By then we care for these people *and* we are hooked by the action.

Here is an exercise that will pay tremendous dividends for you: Go through the first five thousand words of your manuscript and highlight all the material that is explanatory in nature, that tells us things about the character's past.

Then step back and find a way to *withhold* the most important information. I believe in a bit of backstory up front to help us bond with a character, but not in giving us an entire life history. It's a judgment call, but that's what this writing craft is all about. This exercise will help you make an informed choice.

For example:

Rachel had never been the same since her daughter, Tessie, died at age three.

Obviously, this is a major piece of information about Rachel's emotional state. Instead of coming right out and telling us about it, consider showing us something about Rachel that indicates the trauma without revealing its source. For instance in a restaurant scene:

Rachel reached for the teapot. And froze. The tea cozy had a flower pattern on it, the same one—

"What is it?" Mary asked.

Rachel opened her mouth to speak but no words came out. She noticed her hand trembling in mid-air. She withdrew it to her lap. "I'm sorry," she said. "Would you mind pouring?"

Only later will it be revealed that the last time Rachel was with Tessie they'd had a "tea party" with a set that looked exactly like what is on the table at the restaurant.

Look for opportunities to keep readers wondering what the heck is going on—in plot, in character emotions, and in the world of the story itself. If you want to see a master at work on all three levels, read *Rebecca* by Daphne du Maurier, or see the film version directed by Alfred Hitchcock.

Think back on some of your favorite novels. Do they not contain this essential element of mystery in the opening chapters, and even well beyond?

Note: the first part of this post is adapted from *The Art of War for Writers*.

The Two Things Every Novel Needs

"Trouble is my business." — **Raymond Chandler**

So you want to be a writer. You want to sell your novel to a publisher, via an agent, or maybe you're thinking of going indie like 90% of sentient beings these days. Maybe you think if you do the latter, and do it fast, you'll rake in a boatload of easy lettuce.

Well, you won't. Unless your book has the two things every novel needs.

Without these two things, you will have no story. At least, no story most readers will care about. You might have an "experimental novel," and that's okay if you understand what experimental novel means. It means a novel that five people buy. (Please note: This may not matter to you, and that's perfectly fine with me. Experimental artists have given us some good stuff over the years. A lot of bad stuff, too. But if that's your corner of the artistic world, go for it. This is America, after all.)

But if you want to sell your work and have a shot at generating income, you need to master these two elements.

They are *Conflict* and *Suspense.*

Conflict

What is the goal of the novel? Is it to entertain? Teach? Preach? Stir up anger? Change the world? Make the author a lot of money?

It can be any of these things, but in the end, none of these objectives will work to their full potential unless they forge, in some way, *a satisfying emotional experience for the reader.*

And what gets the reader hooked emotionally? *Trouble.* Readers are gripped by the terrible trials a character goes through. (There are psychological reasons for this that are beyond the scope of this section.)

That's where conflict comes in. While there are writers who say plot comes from character, let me say that's too simplistic. Character actually comes from plot. Why? Because *true character is only revealed in crisis.* Put your character into big trouble (plot) and then we'll see what he or she is made of (character). If you don't believe me, imagine a 400 page novel about Scarlett O'Hara where she just sits on the porch all day, sipping mint juleps and flirting. *Gone With the Wind* only takes off when she finds out Ashley is going to marry Melanie (trouble) and then the Civil War breaks out (big trouble!).

Another way to think about it is this: We all wear masks in our lives. A major crisis forces us to take off the mask and reveal who we really are. That's the role of conflict in fiction: to rip the mask off the character.

Now, this conflict must be of sufficient magnitude to matter to readers. That's why I teach that "death stakes" must be involved. Your Lead character must be facing death — which can be physical, professional or psychological.

Genre doesn't matter. In a literary novel like *The Catcher in the Rye,* it's psychological death. Holden Caulfield must find meaning in the world or he will "die inside." Psychological death is also the key to a category romance. If the two lovers do not get together, they will lose their soul mate. They will die inside and forever have diminished lives. (That's the feeling you need to create. Think about it. Why was *Titanic* such a hit with teen girls? It wasn't because of the special effects!)

In *The Silence of the Lambs,* it's professional death on the line. Clarice Starling must help bring down Buffalo Bill in part by playing mind games with Hannibal Lecter. If she doesn't prevail, another innocent will die (physical death in the subplot) and Clarice's career will be over.

And in most thrillers, of course, you have the threat of physical death hanging over the whole thing.

That's why, novelist friend, trouble is indeed your business. Without sufficient conflict readers aren't going to care enough to finish the book.

Suspense

The second element is *suspense,* and I don't just mean in the suspense novel *per se.* Suspense means to "delay resolution so as to excite anticipation." Another way to say this is that it's the opposite of having a predictable story. If the reader keeps guessing what's going to happen, and is right, there is no great pleasure in reading the novel.

We've all had the wonderful experience of being so caught up in a story that we have to keep turning the pages. This is where writing technique can be studied and learned and applied. For example, there are various ways you can end a chapter so readers are compelled to read on. I call these "Read on Prompts," and it was one of the first things I personally studied when I started learning to write. I went to a used bookstore and bought a bunch of King, Koontz and Grisham. When I'd get to the end of a chapter I'd write in pencil on the page what they did to get me to read on.

Invaluable.

Again, genre doesn't matter. You have to be able to excite anticipation and avoid predictability. Suspense technique helps you to do that.

I am so passionate about this that I wrote a whole book on the subject, and Writer's Digest Books published it.

Suffice to say that if you were to concentrate almost exclusively on these two key elements for the next few months, your books will take a huge step toward that exalted "next level" everyone always talks about. Try it and see.

May your own writing year be filled with plenty of conflict and suspense (on the page, I mean!).

Opening No No's

Writer's Digest came out with a special issue some time ago called "Write Your Novel in 30 Days." One section had a collection of things not to do in your opening chapter, based on statements by literary agents. Here are some clips.

Excessive Description

"Slow writing with a lot of description will put me off very quickly," says Andrea Hurst. And this is something you'll hear all the time.

So how do you set an opening scene? Do it with an interplay of action and description. Get the action started first, then fill in just enough information to tell us where we are.

But you're a literary writer, you say? You love style? Well, if you're really good, like Ken Kesey's opening pages in *Sometimes a Great Notion*, go for it. But you can still start with action and drop in wonderful, styling description later.

Voice and Point of View Fuzziness

"A pet peeve of mine is ragged, fuzzy point-of-view," writes Cricket Freeman.

This is especially important when writing in First Person POV. We need voice, we need attitude. Like Holden Caulfield in The Catcher in the Rye or Philip Marlowe in any of Chandler's books. Don't be bland.

Clichés

My friend, agent Chip MacGregor, lists several, including:

1. Squinting into the sunlight with a hangover in a crime novel. Done to death.

2. A trite statement ("Get with the program" or "Houston, we have a problem").

3. Years later, Monica would look back and laugh . . .

4. The [adjective] sun rose in the [adjective] [adjective] sky, shedding its [adjective] light across the [adjective] [adjective] land.

Other Pet Peeves

1. Descriptions making the characters seem too perfect.

2. Too much backstory.

3. Information dumps.

4. A grisly murder scene from the murder scene from the killer's POV.

5. Dreams.

6. Too much exposition in dialogue.

7. Whiny characters.

8. Characters who address the reader directly.

So there you have it, a handy list of no no's in your opening. Does that mean these are "rules"? I know how you rebellious and creative writers hate rules, so no, they aren't. But they will increase your odds of turning off an agent or editor.

So resist the temptation. When you get a deal, then you can fight to begin your novel another way if you see fit.

But first you have to sell, and these bumps will keep you from that goal.

Should Your Series Character Change Over Time?

What do you like to see in a series character? The same

"feel" over and over, or deepening and changing?

There are two schools of thought on this.

Lee Child once remarked that he loves Dom Perignon champagne and wants each bottle to be the same. He's not looking for a different taste each time out. So it is with his Jack Reacher novels. And millions of fans are tracking right along with him.

There are other enduring series where the character remains roughly static. Phillip Marlowe didn't change all that much until *The Long Goodbye*. James Bond? Not a whole lot of change going on inside 007.

At the other end of the spectrum are those characters who undergo significant transformation as the series moves along. The best contemporary example of this is, in my view, the Harry Bosch series by Michael Connelly. What he's done with Bosch from book to book is nothing short of astonishing.

Lawrence Block's Matthew Scudder was traipsing along as a pretty standard PI until Block made a conscious decision to kick it up a notch by going deeper. He did that with *Eight Million Ways to Die*, a book that just knocked me out. Here we have Scudder not just on a new case, but also battling his alcoholism and the existential angst of life in New York City in the early 1980s. By going deeper Block created one of the classics of the genre.

In my Mallory Caine, Zombie-at-Law series (written as K. Bennett) I have a lead character who is a zombie hungering (you'll pardon the phrase) for change. She doesn't want to be what she is. Book 2, *The Year of Eating Dangerously*, begins with Mallory in the hills looking down at a motorcycle gang and thinking, *Lunch*. And then reflecting on her damaged soul.

In the same vein is my series about boxer Irish Jimmy Gallagher. These are short stories, and I'm going for "revealing" more of Jimmy in each one. "Iron Hands" was the intro, giving us Jimmy's world and basic personality. Next was "King Crush."

"King Crush" takes place in 1955 and revolves around an old carnival attraction they used to have in America, the carny fighter who would take on locals. If the locals stayed with him long enough, they might earn back their five bucks and some more besides. But these carny pugs knew all the dirty tricks, and it was usually the hayseeds who ended up on the canvas.

Jimmy just wants to have a good time at the carnival with his girl, Ruby, and his bulldog, Steve. He's not looking for trouble. But sometimes trouble finds Jimmy Gallagher.

I started writing these stories because there's something in me that wants to know Jimmy Gallagher, what makes him tick. And that's my preference as a writer and a reader of series. I want to go a little deeper each time.

When I posted these opinions on the group blog *Kill Zone*, it sparked a lively discussion. Both "sides" were represented.

Writer Basil Sands said, "I like reading series in which the main characters grow and change as the story proceeds. Bernard Cornwall's Richard Sharpe comes to mind. Series with a static character lose my interest pretty quickly for the same reason that I can't usually stick with television series very long. If I know what to expect I get bored quickly, because I can guess the story's end before the halfway point and it loses its fun."

Clare Langley-Hawthorne agreed: "I'm with Basil—I like the characters to change like Richard Sharpe. Still the same inherent guy but after all he's been through he's grown and changed . . . otherwise I find it faintly ridiculous when series characters don't change no matter what is thrown at them."

On the other side, Joe Moore, co-author of the Cotton Stone thrillers, said, "I tend to subscribe to the first school of thought. If I'm into a favorite series, I consider the lead character to be a close friend, and like a friend, I want to feel comfortable with him or her. That doesn't mean total predictability. A surprise or two is what makes the character whole and human. But the series character is the constant for me in each installment of the series. For instance, if I pick up a Cussler novel, I know what to expect from Dirk Pitt. Pitt is not going to change, nor do I want him to. He is what he is. The fact that he doesn't change is what I like about him. No matter what the situation, I can depend on my friend, Mr. Pitt, to do what I expect him to do to get the job done. What makes Pitt appealing is his ability to come up with an original and exciting solution to a unique problem. Cotton Stone is the main series character in my first 4 thrillers. At the end of the final installment, *The 731 Legacy,* Cotton is basically the same person as she was when I introduced her on page 1 of *The Grail Conspiracy.* She has learned a great deal about herself over the arc of the series, but her actions and reactions are rock solid through all 4 books. What my co-writer and I did during the planning stage of each book was to ask: What else does Cotton need to learn? The answer helped to develop the plot, but the knowledge she gained by the end of the story only fortified her already-established character. In my opinion, a series character should be like a favorite, well-worn piece of clothing. When I put it on, it feels good. And when I take it off, I miss the comfort and intimacy, and I look forward to putting it on again."

Joe Hartlaub referenced his own favorite series character, James Lee Burke's Dave Robicheaux. "Burke has walked a fine line with Robicheaux, making changes in his life — and advancing it chronologically — while keeping the core elements of his character intact and consistent. Burke has also advanced Dave's age; there was some concern that THE GLASS RAINBOW would be the last of the Robicheaux novels — Dave apparently having run out of road at the of that book — though that fear has been relieved by the announcement of the publication of CREOLE BELLE this summer. Go Dave! I like stories about old guys who can still kick ass and take names!"

The topic of "aging" the character then came up. Is it better to leave age out of it? Or, like Connelly with Bosch, age the character in "real time"?

John Gilstrap had a strong opinion on that. "I deliberately

keep Jonathan Grave ageless in the series. We know he's war-weary, and that he's been around the block a few times, but I see no need to nail his age to a specific decade. I know from fan mail, for example, that younger readers see him younger than I do, and that's fine with me. In any given book, the secondary characters — the ones Jonathan is saving — develop on a much sharper arc than the recurring characters do. That said, I make it a point in each book to reveal to the reader a little bit more about what makes Jonathan the kind of man he is. One thing he is not is introspective. As he says at the end of HOSTAGE ZERO, those doors in his mind are locked for a reason."

Jordan Dane felt that the Lucas Davenport series, by John Sanford, suffered with the aging of the character, and his marriage, which seemed to make him too "domesticated" and different from the "bad boy" she liked in the earlier works.

This caused me to reflect: "I heard Michael Connelly talk once about his decision to age Bosch in 'real time.' That is, he is 20 years older today than he was in 1992. It has worked magnificently, but it also presents Connelly with bittersweet challenges, he said. Bosch is closing in on retirement age, for example. How will that affect the dynamics of the story? Connelly wasn't sure. Perhaps like Block's Scudder, who also has aged, the added years bring him more wisdom in his pursuits. But it also helps that these two authors are just flat out so good that they can render the inner life just as effectively as the outer. Jordan mentions Lucas Davenport and not tracking with age thing. Maybe a difference between a Davenport and a Bosch is that the former is more 'actiony.' More physical.

Like Reacher, part of the delight is the kicking butt part. So in that sense, the aging could dilute that part of the experience. What do you think? One of the benefits of doing a HISTORICAL series character, which Jimmy Gallagher is, is that I can take whatever time I want. Right now he's in 1955, and I'm in no rush to get him into the 1960s!"

I added another thought about interiority and "angst" in a series character: "Mike Hammer was the hardest of the hardboiled, but Mickey Spillane does have a few sections where Hammer really chews himself out—he's a killer because of what he went through in WWII, and conflicted and driven at the same time. These passages are compellingly written."

Jordan Dane responded: "As for internalizing, I think less is more. Pepper it in and don't keep repeating the same point. Within each scene, I try to advance the character's awareness from the start of a scene with different points towards the end so it shows movement in motivation. I think over-angsty comes from repeating points ad nauseum."

So there we have it. A pretty even split, but where aging is involved be especially careful. Think through your series before you begin, at least on this score. How much transformation will there be? Are you more into character-driven or plot-driven fiction? If the former, change may be the ticket. If the latter, perhaps not so much.

There are readers for both kinds of stories, so don't sweat it too much. Write what you'd like to read.

Incite This

Among writing instructors you'll often hear the term "inciting incident." It's part of the craft jargon. I've never liked it. In fact, I think I've only used it once or twice in the past, and then only to make some minor point about something else.

But now it's time to dump it completely.

For starters, no one agrees on a definition. Is it the "action that starts the story" or the "Call to Adventure"? Is it the scene that "kicks the story into motion"? And if it is, what is all that stuff BEFORE the "inciting incident"? Stuff that DOESN'T kick the story into motion? Every scene in your book or movie better incite SOMETHING or it shouldn't be there.

Is it an "event that forces the hero to react"? But there are many events that force reaction in a novel. If there aren't, you've got a four-letter novel, spelled d-u-l-l.

Is the "inciting incident" supposed to happen near the opening of the novel? Or is it the break into Act 2? You'll find it given both ways.

Does the inciting incident "upset the balance of forces in the protagonist's life"?

Well, if it does, how come it's only *one* incident? There are *lots of incidents in a story that upset the "balance of forces."*

Look at *The Wizard of Oz*. Miss Gulch takes Toto away. Dorothy gets him back and runs away. A twister hits and carries her to Oz. She meets a bunch of Munchkins and a good witch who looks like a soap bubble. She's confronted by the Wicked Witch and threatened with death. Then she's given the ruby slippers and told to follow the yellow brick road. She meets three odd allies, is peppered with apples by angry trees, gets intimidated by the Great Oz, gets carried away by flying monkeys and imprisoned, disposes of the Wicked Witch, gets cheated by Oz (until Toto reveals the man behind the curtain) and ends up back in black and white Kansas.

All of those incidents "upset the balance of forces."

"Inciting incident" explains nothing. Throw it out like yesterday's French onion soup.

Instead, think of it this way. You open with a disturbance. That's change or challenge, anything that puts a ripple in the Lead's ordinary life.

How does *The Wizard of Oz* start? Not with a rainbow, or birds singing, or Dorothy waking up happy. No. The first shot is her running down the road, afraid of Miss Gulch coming after Toto.

Then we get to the Act 1 break. This I call the Doorway of No Return. It's got to force the Lead through and slam shut. That's what Act 2 has to feel like. The Lead is in the trouble and has to solve it. She can't go running back to the placid world where she came from.

The twister in *Oz* does that to Dorothy. The murder of his Aunt and Uncle does that to Luke Skywalker. Life will never be the same for them.

Now some writers have these ideas right in their DNA and do these things instinctively. Others have to learn how to do them. Still others, even published authors, could strengthen their books by giving these craft points some thought.

I urge all writers to keep up a study of the craft. Would you want your brain surgery to be done by a doctor who is reading the medical journals and constantly trying to improve? Or the one who has just returned from a year-long vacation in Barbados, where he did nothing but lounge on the beach sipping Piña Coladas?

Writing is like brain surgery, except nobody dies when you make a mistake.

Limit the Exposition in Your Opening Pages

On the blog The Kill Zone, we sometimes invite people to submit for public consumption their opening pages. We then offer them a critique of same. This one came in for me, and I thought it led to an important point. I'll give the opening, then my comments:

Z.O.M.B.I.E. Squad: Hot ZOMBIE Nights

Jaz surveyed the semi-dark alley after escaping from her

BMW. Drat. ZOMBIES. Not what she needed at the moment. How would she explain this to her new boyfriend? Not the ZOMBIES per se, but the fact that this would be the third time this week that she'd bailed on dinner with him. Well, if he was a quality catch, he'd let her make it up to him, if not, there were other non-ZOMBIES out there in the world. Right?

There was a screech of metal on metal, as one of the ZOMBIEs dragged something along the side of her M3, and it would definitely leave a mark. Ok, "drat" just officially became "double-damn" the minute both her love life and her car became casualties. Being undercover with ZOMBIE International Technologies was never easy. Often it downright stunk, just like this alley. It always seemed to be us or them and just a street away from normal. Whoever thought that all aliens were smarter and more techno-savvy, never met a pod-ZOMBIE.

The pod-Zs looked almost as unearthly as they were. Jaz could see their sallow, waxy faces as they stepped out of the shadows and into the moonlight. Light-colored images of the humans they might have been. Ok, maybe she could see why someone who didn't know better might think they were just the walking. Jaz's chest heaved a bit as she took in one, deep, cleansing breath. It was warm, wet, and tasted a bit like the Cuban carne asada she'd planned on having for dinner. She sighed as she pulled the transonic pen-dart from her bra: her $100 Dior Du jour, lace alternative, super-sexy, continental blue bra, with matching underwear. Yes, they did match her Beemer perfectly. That should say something about the level of clothing perfection and date desirability she had worked so hard for as she prepared to meet up with 3DP-vid god, Wylie Taylor.

It pained her to risk her Dior bra by using it as a weapon holder, but without stockings, there were few choices to secure a pen-sized super weapon and keep it accessible.

****

Paranormal fiction. Zombies. You have to build a world, and that's what the writer is attempting to do here, plus give us exposition to boot. And the instincts are good: weave the exposition within the action.

However, this opening is weighted too heavily on the informational (notice how "blocky" the text is on the page). It's a common mistake made because the writer feels the reader has to be clued in to a lot of background before he can understand what's going on.

Almost always a wrong choice. Because readers will *wait a long time* for explanations so long as *something is happening that is disturbing.*

This first page delivers a great opening disturbance. To make it even more effective, let the action be primary and drop exposition in later, a bit at a time.

To show you what I mean, here is the opening rendered with just the action sentences:

Jaz surveyed the semi-dark alley after escaping from her

BMW. There was a screech of metal on metal, as one of the ZOMBIEs dragged something along the side of the M3.

She could see their sallow, waxy faces as they stepped out of the shadows and into the moonlight. Light-colored images of the humans they might have been.

She sighed as she pulled the transonic pen-dart from her bra.

****

I am much more in this scene now. I want to keep reading. I want to know what that thing in her bra does.

The author has me hooked, and can begin to drop in exposition *as needed.* But keep it brief. The next lines might be:

Being undercover with ZOMBIE International Technologies was never easy. Often it downright stunk, just like this alley.

Then get back to the action. Then later the stuff about the boyfriend. More action. And so on.

Also, I'd cut: **The pod-Zs looked almost as unearthly as they were.** This is a "tell" just before the "show" of the next sentence. The latter creates a picture for the reader, who can then draw his own conclusion.

I like the voice that is "lurking" here. But it sounds "once removed," e.g. in this line: **That should say something about the level of clothing perfection and date desirability she had worked so hard for as she prepared to meet up with 3DP-vid god, Wylie Taylor.**

This is the author commenting on Jaz, not something from Jaz herself. I wonder if the author might consider turning this into a First Person narration. Then the fun aspects of the voice could come out more naturally, e.g.:

I pulled the transonic pen-dart from my $100 Dior Du jour, lace alternative, super-sexy, continental blue bra, with matching underwear. Matched my Beemer, too. But this was about date desirability. Hard work, but then again it was 3DP-vid god Wylie Taylor I was going to meet up with.

If I ever got away from these Zs.

That's just a suggestion, something to consider. One can achieve pretty much the same effect in Third Person, but should make sure the narration sounds like thoughts your character would actually think, and keep author commentary out of it.

I like this concept. Hey, fun zombie thrillers are my bag. So hook me with action in this first chapter and drop in *only the exposition that is absolutely, positively necessary for the understanding of the scene.*

It is much less than you think. And a much better start without it.

Is "Show, Don't Tell" Overrated?

A well-known author (whom I like personally and admire professionally) is of the opinion that "show, don't tell" is an overrated bit of advice. He believes there's nothing wrong with telling a great deal of a story in the author's voice.

So let's talk about that a bit.

Here is an excerpt from a thriller which begins in the trenches of WWI. After a descriptive opening paragraph that introduces us to the "cordite-clouded sky" and the lead character, Dr. William T. Majors, Jr., we get this:

A brilliant mathematician, Majors was a scholar and a gentleman completely out of his affluent Long Island element. Against reasonable odds or definable logic, he was also a private in the U.S. Army and at present trapped in a gash of dangerous dirt between France and Germany known as the Western Front.

That is narrative telling and setup. Well, why not? It gets the job done, doesn't it?

But wouldn't we rather be in the head of the character, and let the details become known naturally as we go along? Is there a need to explain all this up front? Does it deepen our involvement, distance it, or matter not at all?

I have a little guideline I call *Act first, explain later.* I have never read the opening of a published book yet that did not benefit from this guideline, or suffer from its non-use.

Side note: I was talking to a friend recently who is a voracious reader (and was a history major in college). I brought up a particularly popular series of historical novels and he went, "Ugh! It takes SO LONG to get going!" Then he mentioned the James Clavell classic, *Shogun.* "He gives a lot of background," my friend said, "but he does it with action. I like that much better." I try to listen to readers.

Back to the thriller. We are now introduced to a second character, Majors' childhood friend, John Taylor. They enlisted together. They are in the trench, talking as the sky explodes. "Tell me again," Taylor says, "what the hell we are doing here?"

Then this:

Both men were scared, though they tried not to show it.

They winced, recoiling again from the thundering bombardment now under way to destroy fortifications and trench systems along a twenty-mile front from Bois d'Avoncourt to Étan.

Okay, that is a pull back from a *scene* (when there's dialogue, you've got a scene by default) to *narrative description.* The author is telling us what *both* men felt, so it's author voice (and therefore Omniscient POV) by default.

Are we okay with that? Or would it not be better to stay within the POV of Majors, his hands shaking, the bile of fear rising in his throat? (Note: Omniscient POV is out of favor these days.)

A novel works best (even, I am tempted to add, *only*) when it *creates emotion in the reader*. One of the reasons for *show, don't tell* is to do that very thing. And it ought to start happening on page one.

A few lines down (we're on page 2 now), Majors has a tender moment:

Majors touched his heart, then pulled a photo of Jane from his tunic's breast pocket. He could make out her features in the sudden glare of a bomb's blast. He loved her deeply and felt this was probably his last chance to look upon her face.

More telling. But does *He loved her deeply* capture the feeling? Or would it have been better to *show* his finger gently tracing her features as his heart pounds something that sounds like a dirge? *Telling* us what an emotion is, rather than *creating it in us*, wastes valuable front-end real estate in a book.

Now a page of backstory follows. It begins:

Even more than Taylor, Majors had been born and raised in privilege, with every advantage of wealth and sophistication his parents could give him. Majors' father, the man he'd been named after, was a successful ship line attorney and investment banker. Majors' French mother had always been a tender caregiver to her son. She was a consummate homemaker and devoted wife . . .

We have left the immediacy of the action and exploding sky for a discursive on background. Now, I believe some backstory is all right in an opening chapter. But I like to keep it brief and firmly grounded in a character's head and emotions, e.g., *He longed to be back in his father's study, helping him research another brief for the shipping lines he represented, waiting for mother to bring the afternoon tea.*

Is there ever a time to just "tell" part of the story? Yes, when you want to get from point A to point B in the least amount of time, e.g., from one location to another.

Otherwise, choose the more intimate way, one character's immediate POV, and create emotions rather than telling us about them.

Give Us Attitude in First Person POV

Here is the first page of an unpublished novel, submitted anonymously to *The Kill Zone* blog for analysis:

The surveillance van stank. That wasn't unusual. Put two or more people in a confined space for hours on end and the scent fallout will inevitably be a combination of stale sweat and Funyuns with the desperate hint of pine from a cardboard tree hanging on the rearview mirror.

". . . so I told her that's how it would be irregardless of what she wanted," Johnson said.

The words registered, but I hadn't paid the slightest attention to the context. "Uh huh."

"You're a woman, what do you think the problem is?"

"I don't know. Your use of the non-word irregardless?"

Surveillance work was the closest I'd been to the field since being shot three months earlier. I thought it would be better than desk duty. I was wrong.

I popped the lid off a bottle of ibuprofen and dry swallowed three. Getting shot hurt. What was done to keep me alive hurt more. The company in the van and our location wasn't helping. Ed Kowalczyk once wrote a song called "Shit Towne," about York, Pennsylvania. I've been to York. Ed wrote a good song. He needs to write one about Reading.

"Do I have to go outside?" asked Johnson, changing topics. At least, I thought that's what he was doing.

"What?"

"When I'm on surveillance with a guy," he put too much emphasis on that gender specific word, "I can just pee out the back door of the van."

"If I see your penis, I will shoot it," I said.

He grumbled, but left in search of a public restroom, or a bush. I didn't care as long as the smell from the contents of his bladder didn't reach my nose.

****

JSB: The voice of the narrator in this piece is strong. When writing in First Person, that's the main goal. Give us an *attitude.* The narrator should sound like someone specific, and someone who might be worth listening to.

This narrator has a good, irreverent, spunky style. We like protagonists who have a bit of the rebel in them. Why? Because that promises conflict, which is the engine of fiction. In that regard, the repartee is promising. We know this Lead is going to run afoul of those she has to work with.

I also like the crisp attention to detail. The *desperate hint of pine from a cardboard tree* is excellent. And it's mixed with Funyuns (note: capitalize product names). That's specific. It's almost always better to use actual names than generic categories.

The main way I'd strengthen this opening is to root us in the POV right from the start. I see this kind of opening a lot—a sensory description, but from a voice we have not identified yet. Could this be the author's omniscient voice? A third person "in the head" voice? Or is this First Person? If so, who is the person?

We don't get clued in until the third paragraph.

Thus, I strongly urge writers to make that opening paragraph clear about the POV. My suggested reworking is below. It's by no means the only way, but it'll give you an idea of what I mean.

****

I popped the lid off a bottle of ibuprofen and dry

swallowed three. Getting shot hurt. What was done to keep me alive hurt more.

". . . so I told her that's how it would be irregardless of what she wanted," Johnson said.

The words registered, but I hadn't paid the slightest attention to the context. "Uh huh."

"You're a woman, what do you think the problem is?"

"I don't know. Your use of the non-word irregardless?"

The surveillance van stank. That wasn't unusual. Put two or more people in a confined space for hours on end and the scent fallout will inevitably be a combination of stale sweat and Funyuns with the desperate hint of pine from a cardboard tree hanging on the rearview mirror.

Surveillance work was the closest I'd been to the field since being shot three months earlier. I thought it would be better than desk duty. I was wrong . . . .

****

JSB: Now, I know the thinking is that the author wants to establish the setting first, the van, then get to the scene. But readers will wait for setting information if something is happening, like dialogue with a little spice. So putting in description *after* action is often the better choice for the opening page.

Establishing POV and voice right away are:

Janet Evanovich in *Two for the Dough*:

> I knew Ranger was beside me because I could see his
> earring gleaming in the moonlight.

James M. Cain, *The Postman Always Rings Twice*:

> They threw me off the hay truck about noon.

J. D. Salinger, *The Catcher in the Rye*:

> If you really want to hear about it, the first thing
> you'll probably want to know is where I was born,
> and what my lousy childhood was like, and how my
> parents were occupied and all before they had me,
> and all that David Copperfield kind of crap, but I
> don't feel like going into it, if you want to know the
> truth.

And so on. I know immediately we are in First Person, and
that lets me understand better the descriptions that follow,
because it's coming through a particular perspective. And
there is an attitude apparent in each narration as they
move along.

Main point: It's the voice of the narrator that's the number
one thing I look for in First Person.

Dialogue as Weapon

Words hurt.

We've all experienced the stab of pain that comes from an unkind comment or outright insult. Especially if it's from a friend or loved one.

I could never buy into "Sticks and stones may break my bones, but words will never hurt me." Nice try, but it doesn't cut it. Words wound. They have power.

Which is why I've found it helpful to think about dialogue as a weapon. First, it helps us see dialogue as part of overall conflict. And second, it reminds us that all dialogue should be intentional on the part of the character.

John Howard Lawson, a well-known playwright and screenwriter of the mid-20th century, called dialogue "a compression and extension of action." Every word of dialogue from any character in any scene should be uttered to advance his or her agenda.

Example: John D. MacDonald's classic *The Executioners* (basis for the two *Cape Fear* movies) is about a lawyer, Sam Bowden, whose family is stalked by the sadistic rapist Max Cady. Cady's first act is poisoning the family dog, Marilyn. Sam has not been totally up front with his wife, Carol. She challenges him:

> **"I'm not a child and I'm not a fool and I resent being . . . overprotected."**

Her volley is direct, telling him she *resents* the coddling. Sam responds:

> **"I should have told you. I'm sorry."**

Sam's apology is meant to diminish his wife's anger. But his words ring hollow to her, and she continues to advance:

> "So now this Cady can roam around at will and poison our dog and work his way up to the children. Which do you think he'll start on first? The oldest or the youngest?"

> "Carol, honey. Please."

> "I'm a hysterical woman? You are so damn right. I am a hysterical woman."

Sam the lawyer tries a little legal reasoning:

> "We haven't any proof it was Cady."

> She threw a towel into the sink. "Listen to me. *I* have proof it was Cady. I've got that proof. It's not the kind of proof you would like. No evidence. No testimony. Nothing legalistic. I just *know*."

Seeing that this has no effect on her husband, Carol brings out her heavy artillery:

> "What kind of a man are you? This is your *family*. Marilyn was part of your *family*. Are you going to look up all the precedents and prepare a brief?"

She has attacked both his manhood and his profession. Sam attempts an answer but Carol cuts him off (interruptions are good weapons, too):

> "You don't know how—"

"I don't know anything. This is happening because of something you did a long time ago."

"Something I had to do."

"I'm not saying you shouldn't have. You tell me the man hates you. You don't think he's sane. So *do* something about him!"

Carol wants instant action and Sam knows he can't provide it. The stress of the situation brings out weapon-like dialogue.

But you don't need high conflict for characters to use dialogue as weapon. Little jabs can be administered at any time. Here are some ways:

Avoid a direct answer:

"Are you ready to go dear?" John said.
"I saw you downtown today," Mary said.

Answer a question with a question:

"Are you ready to go dear?" John said.
"Why must you always do that?" Mary said.

Use silence:

"Are you ready to go dear?" John said.
Mary said nothing.

Use action beats:

"Are you ready to go dear?" John said.

Mary removed her pearl necklace and tossed it on the dresser.

The characters do not have to be enemies to use dialogue as a weapon. They just have to want different things.

In William E. Barrett's *The Lilies of the Field,* a German nun wants wandering handyman Homer Smith to stay and build a chapel for her small order. He just wants to get paid for the work he's done and move on. He confronts Mother Maria Marthe:

> **"I want to talk to you," he said. "I've been doing work for you. Good work. I want pay for what I do."**
>
> **She sat silent, with her hands clasped in front of her. Her small eyes looked at him out of the wrinkled mask of her face but there was no light in them. He did not know whether she understood him or not.**

After the silent treatment, Homer decides to play hardball. He directs the nun to a Bible verse, *The labourer is worthy of his hire,* and explains, "I'm a poor man. I work for wages."

Not to be outdone, and using the same weapon, Mother Maria Marthe shows Homer another passage: *And why take ye thought for raiment? Consider the lilies of the field, how they grow; they toil not, neither do they spin. And yet I say unto you that even Solomon in all his glory was not arrayed like one of these.*

Homer realizes he is dealing with one crafty nun who has won the initial tussle.

Review your dialogue exchanges from each character's POV, asking yourself how they might use every line of their dialogue as a way to get what they want. If that's not clear to you, cut that line or rewrite it.

You'll be pleased at how much sharper and more readable your dialogue will be.

How to "Steal" Plots

The secret to creativity is knowing how to hide your sources. – Albert Einstein

A creative exercise I have suggested in workshops is "stealing" old plots to generate new story ideas. I have occasionally heard an objection to this, that it might in some way "unethical" or show a lack of original thinking.

If so, the greatest literary felon of all time is a hack named William Shakespeare. Most of his plays were lifted from other sources.

For example, Bill used an obscure narrative poem entitled *The Tragical History of Romeus and Juliet* as the basis for his play. He didn't even change the names of the titular characters! What cheek! Which reminds me: Wasn't there someone who had the bright idea of "stealing" the plot of *Romeo and Juliet* and turning it into a Broadway musical? I believe his name was Jerome Robbins and the musical was something with the word *West* in the title. Ha ha, nice try. We could see right through that!

I once read a thriller about a small town where people were being transformed into animal-like creatures who feasted on human flesh. One of the characters in the town, a child, was convinced her parents were not really her parents anymore.

As I read that I thought of one of my favorite movies, *Invasion of the Body Snatchers* (the 1956 version). At the beginning of the movie a little boy is running away from his mother because he doesn't believe she's his mother anymore.

And I'm thinking, this novelist is obviously borrowing from the movie.

Then a bit later in the novel, it's revealed that the animal-people are the result of biological experiments by a mad genius.

And now I'm thinking, the author has borrowed H.G. Welles's plot for *The Island of Dr. Moreau.*

The clever scribe had purloined not just one plot, but two!

I thought I'd caught this author, but then he gave me one

last twist. He had a character think that the whole thing reminded him of *Invasion of the Body Snatchers*, and later on another referred to *The Island of Dr. Moreau.*

He was winking at readers like me and all those who knew exactly what he was doing!
And this author does know what he's doing. His name is Dean Koontz. The book is *Midnight.*

Here is the point. It is perfectly acceptable to take an old plot and update it, or combine it with another plot and come up with something fresh. That's all originality is, by the way. It's taking old stuff and looking at it in a new way. I use the word "steal" with tongue in cheek, of course (as did an old writer's book *Steal This Plot).* This is just a creative exercise that works nicely if you keep the following guidelines in mind:

1. Don't Plagiarize

Getting ideas from a plot is not plagiarism, so long as you are not copying actual passages from the book. In 2011 Little, Brown just pulled a book from distribution when it was found that the author had lifted material directly from James Bond novels and other sources. In an ironic twist, the book's ranking on Amazon shot up as readers snapped up the remaining copies. This is not a marketing move I would recommend.

Plagiarism is thievery, pure and simple. If you do that you're a pirate, not a writer.

2. Make the Plot Your Own

I would not recommend that you write a novel about a spoiled, antebellum girl on the cusp of the Civil War, who wants to marry a handsome Southerner pledged to another, and at the same time she is courted by a dashing rogue. But the love triangle from *Gone With the Wind* could work perfectly well in a future world where intergalactic war is about to break out.

You see the point? The "stealing" of a plot idea is only meant to open up a window to new possibilities. You still need to create your own characters and bring a personal passion to the story.

3. Use Plot Elements as Sparkers

You don't need to follow a plot pattern wholesale to find this exercise of value. You can use plot elements, characters and scenes and riff off them. We do that anyway, unconsciously. When you see a film or read a book and are moved by something, it gets sent down to the basement where your writer's unconscious mind is eating a sandwich. Later on, your sub-mind looks it over and either files it away or sends up a message recommending you do something with it. Sometimes you may not even remember the source as a fresh idea takes hold. This is all natural and acceptable.

So why not be intentional about it? Keep notes on elements that work for you, and why they work. File those away and look them over occasionally. See what bubbles up.
One caveat: A great plot *twist* requires special care. I mean,

what about the jaw dropping reveal in *The Sixth Sense?* **Spoiler Alert!** You can't really do a story about a doctor helping a kid who sees dead people, who then turns out to be dead himself, without incurring wrath and scorn. But you might be able to find another supernatural twist with just as much impact. Use your common sense here. Do not give your dying old man a childhood sled named *Rosebud.*

So go ahead and utilize old plots to help you make up something new. Shakespeare would approve, and so would Koontz and scores of well-known writers who have done exactly the same thing over the years.

How I Went From Idea to Story

I wrote a novella called *One More Lie.* I thought it might be instructive to describe the process I used to come up with it.

There are various creative exercises I use to come up with story possibilities. One of my favorites is the first line game. You make up a bunch of intriguing first lines all at once and see where they lead. I learned this from Dean Koontz in his classic *How to Write Bestselling Fiction.* Koontz himself once wrote the line: *"You ever killed anything?" Roy asked.* He didn't know anything else, but the line grabbed him and eventually he fleshed it out to the novel *The Voice of the Night.*

For *One More Lie*, I actually got a first *chapter* idea. So I wrote it. I liked it so much I put it in my "active file" to noodle on later.

It stayed there for about a year as I worked on other projects, primarily those for which I had been paid, the publishers having the perfectly quaint notion that I therefore owed them a book.

But every now and again I'd return to that opening and think about it.

The day came when I had a window of time and decided to give it a whirl. So what I did was this:

1. Fleshed out the main characters. In this case there were four, and I spent time coming up with relationships and backstory. That in turn suggested further plot developments. I call this "orchestration" and it's one of the most important things a writer can do with a new idea.

2. I experimented with POV. I had originally written the opening in third person. Sometimes I'll switch POV to see how it feels. In this case, I decided that First Person was a better fit. My previous novella, *Watch Your Back*, was written in that sort of James M. Cain style I like, so I went with the same for *One More Lie*.

3. I let the plot unfold as I wrote, but took notes and outlined as I went. This is a "rolling outline" that enables you to think ahead during the writing process itself. It allows a certain freedom in plot while at the same time you're building a solid structure. One benefit is that a particular twist happened out of the blue that completely changed the direction of the story and gave it the deeper

dimension I was looking for.

4. I completed a first draft, let it sit, then printed it out in hard copy for my first read-through. I take minimal notes at this stage, wanting to have a "reading experience" first. Then I assessed the big picture and revised it.

5. I gave it to my beta readers, starting with my lovely wife, who has a great editorial eye. I got terrific notes back. One of the readers did the copy edit for me.

6. I prepared it for e-publication, sent it out to be formatted. My son wanted to take a stab at designing the cover, and who was I to argue? The price was right. As in zip.

7. My son, a film grad, also did the trailer, posted on YouTube. For that I bought him dinner.

And then the book was ready for publication. Once I started writing it, it took about two months for publication.

The Importance of Concept

I was going through some old files the other day and came across a little scrap of paper from several years ago. I remember it well. I was on a trip to talk with my publisher at the time, Zondervan. I was preparing the pitch for my next project, and as I always try to do, wanted to get it into pristine form.

I had an idea that had been chugging around my brain awhile. It was based on two things. First, an uncomfortable encounter with someone from my past who was insistent on edging back into my life.

The other was the plot of one of my favorite novels, *The Executioners* by John D. MacDonald (basis of the *Cape Fear* films).

I put those two items together. This is a great method of coming up with plot ideas, by the way. Dean Koontz has been a master at this. For instance, *Midnight,* one of his best thrillers, is a cross between *Invasion of the Body Snatchers* and *The Island of Dr. Moreau.* Koontz even references those titles in the book itself, to "wink" at the readers who recognize the plotlines! But all the characters and the setting are new, original creations. That's how that's done.

Anyway, I was in the hotel room in Grand Rapids and jotted this:

How far will a man go to protect his family? For lawyer Sam Trask, it's farther than he ever thought possible. Because when an unwelcome presence from his past comes calling, bent on the destruction of his family, Sam must leave the civilized corners of the law and journey into the heart of darkness.

Not bad for an on-the-spot jot on Holiday Inn note paper. The concept was the basis of my novel *No Legal Grounds* (2007), which became a bestseller and is still one of my favorite thrillers.

The reason: concept. If you don't get your concept solid

and simple from the start, you're likely to wander around in soggy bogs and down random rabbit trails.

A writing teacher once told me that the most successful movies and books were *simple plots about complex characters*. I think he has something there. You should be able to articulate your concept in a couple of lines.

A self-centered Southern belle is forced to fight for her home during and after the Civil War, even as she fights off the charms of a handsome rogue who looks almost exactly like Clark Gable.

To get back home, a Kansas farm girl has to kill a wicked witch in a land full of Munchkins and flying monkeys. Aided by a scarecrow, a tin man and a lion with issues, she faces dangers aplenty along a yellow brick road.

A simple summary like this is your anchor, your floodlight in the darkness. It will keep you focused and writing scenes with organic unity.

In real estate, it's location, location, location.

In fiction, it's concept, concept, concept.

Make sure you know yours before you start writing.

****

After posting this on the Kill Zone blog, I got a comment that asked if this was the same thing as "high concept." My answer:

What I'm talking about here is the concrete, honed idea for

the writer, so he knows the solid through line of the story. The Hollywood idea of a "high concept" is one that I call the "ka-ching ka-ching test." In other words, we see the market from the idea alone. But a concept might be a little "softer."

Thus: A girl whose mother is imprisoned for murder must grow stronger through a series of foster homes. (*White Oleander*). That's simple and complete without necessarily being a "high" concept.

How about this one: The King of England must give a speech, but he has a speech impediment. Through the support of his wife and a quirky speech therapist, he makes it. That doesn't exactly set off the cash register sound, does it? But remember: simple plots and complex characters. *The King's Speech* was so good because of the character work and how the stakes of the speech were raised in the plot.

So the main idea of my post is that the writer be clear about the concept. Excited about it. And then people it with great characters.

Adding Fireworks

The only people for me are the mad ones, the ones who are mad to live, mad to talk, mad to be saved, desirous of everything at the same time, the ones who never yawn or say a commonplace thing, but burn, burn, burn, like fabulous yellow roman candles exploding like spiders across the stars and in the middle you see the blue centerlight pop and everybody goes "Awww!"

The above quote is from a novel published in 1957, a novel that still sells tens of thousands of copies a year. It's *On the Road* by Jack Kerouac, and not only is that clip about fireworks, it demonstrates the power of "fireworks" in fiction. It's the kind of heat and heart that makes for an unforgettable reading experience.

This is the elusive concept called *voice*. It's something agents and editors all talk about, but no one seems able to define. They just know it when they see it. And so do readers.

It's the kind of writing that makes them all go "Awww!"

How can you get that into your fiction? As Red Smith, the famous sportswriter, once said, "There's nothing to writing. You just sit down at a typewriter and open a vein."

It's a matter of having "skin in the game." Of having a heart for your material. If you don't feel it, you're not going to get the reader to feel it.

But to the feeling you must add the craft. Sometimes writers get this wrong. They think because they have a "message" they strongly believe in, or a concept that gets them excited, that's enough to go on.

It's not. You must translate that into a story readers can relate to, and that's what the craft—plot, structure, characters, dialogue, description—is about.

If you put it all together you get the spark that can ignite fireworks.

Let the show begin.

Writing Advice from John Steinbeck

What follows is some writing wisdom via John Steinbeck, from an old interview in *The Paris Review*. Here it is, with some editorial comments tossed in:

Now let me give you the benefit of my experience in facing 400 pages of blank stock—the appalling stuff that must be filled. I know that no one really wants the benefit of anyone's experience which is probably why it is so freely offered. But the following are some of the things I have had to do to keep from going nuts.

1. Abandon the idea that you are ever going to finish. Lose track of the 400 pages and write just one page for each day, it helps. Then when it gets finished, you are always surprised.

JSB: I like this. It's similar to what Ann Lamott counsels in *Bird by Bird,* i.e., the "one inch frame." Just face your daily writing, with full attention. If you do this daily (or at least regularly) at some point you'll look up and see a full novel. I look back over 17 years of getting paid for this, and see over 25 novels. Yes, I'm surprised. But not shocked.

2. Write freely and as rapidly as possible and throw the

whole thing on paper. Never correct or rewrite until the whole thing is down. Rewrite in process is usually found to be an excuse for not going on. It also interferes with flow and rhythm which can only come from a kind of unconscious association with the material.

JSB: I completely agree. I am an outliner (to a degree) but once I get going, I want to finish that first draft as rapidly as I competently can. I edit my previous day's work and then move on. I don't do substantial edits, with one exception. At about 20,000 words I'll stop and assess the foundations of my story (using my LOCK System from *Plot & Structure*). I don't want to press on for another 70k or 80k if the spine is not strong.

3. Forget your generalized audience. In the first place, the nameless, faceless audience will scare you to death and in the second place, unlike the theater, it doesn't exist. In writing, your audience is one single reader. I have found that sometimes it helps to pick out one person—a real person you know, or an imagined person and write to that one.

JSB: I've heard this advice before, but I've never been able to use it. I don't think about readers when I write. I think about the characters. I think about the readers when I *plan*. I make sure I've got a concept that will appeal to people who have discretionary income to spend on books. But once I've put that concept into motion in a novel, I'm involved only with the characters and how they get out of trouble.

4. If a scene or a section gets the better of you and you still

think you want it—bypass it and go on. When you have finished the whole you can come back to it and then you may find that the reason it gave trouble is because it didn't belong there.

JSB: This is good advice, so long as you're not doing it *a lot*. If you do, there's going to be a much bigger mess at the end than there was at the beginning. If you have too many scenes that are not "working," the problem may be in the structural foundations or in scene writing itself.

5. Beware of a scene that becomes too dear to you, dearer than the rest. It will usually be found that it is out of drawing.

JSB: Does anybody know what "out of drawing" means?

6. If you are using dialogue—say it aloud as you write it. Only then will it have the sound of speech.

JSB: I much prefer to write dialogue as it flows, so long as I've used my Voice Journal to really hear the characters. The Voice Journal is a free-form document, where the character talks in his or her own voice to me. I just keep adding to it until the voice becomes unique. When I edit the dialogue, that's when I might say it out loud, or have Word read it to me.

So there you have it. Follow Steinbeck's advice and you might win a Nobel Prize, too.

Or, if not, at least take your writing to a higher plane.

The Flashback Quagmire

Here was another anonymous first page submitted to *The Kill Zone* for critique:

****

Bobby was at a dead sprint when the first bullet hit him in the kidney. He went down hard face first on the concrete and fought to catch his breath. He'd never been in so much pain, but the adrenaline coursing through him forced him to his knees and back to his feet. He was bleeding badly, and his breath came in ragged gasps. He knew he was about to die but couldn't bring himself to stop running.

The rotted corpse of Holy Cross High School, vacant for decades, loomed in front of him. If he could reach the school he might be able to hide from the men hunting him and die in relative peace. God only knew what they had in mind for him if they caught him.

Another shot was fired, but didn't hit him. He knew he'd be easy to track with the amount of blood he was losing. He was growing light headed and his vision was clouding. He was struck by a sudden sadness at the thought of never seeing his family again, and wished he'd listened to his father when he told him to stay the hell out of New Orleans.

Hours earlier, Bobby was laughing and drinking beer in Johnny White's bar on Bourbon Street. A natural extrovert, he did his best to keep a low profile but he couldn't help chatting up some of the more attractive clientele. He never even noticed the young guy with a buzz cut watching him from across the bar.

The buzz cut didn't miss a trick. He watched Bobby drink several beers, make time with a couple of vacationing coeds, and then settle his tab with a Kennedy half dollar. He made a note of the bartender's name, and debated whether to include it in his After Action Report. It was handy to know who did business with freebooters in New Orleans, after all.

As Bobby was leaving the bar, the buzz cut bumped into him and apologized. It never occurred to Bobby that the stranger who bumped him planted an infrared tracking device on him. From then it was just a matter of time.

****

Let me say a couple of things about the first three paragraphs.

Our POV character in this scene is Bobby. And he's been shot. He's on the run. We have a chance, then, to become bonded to Bobby and his plight right away.

That's why I need to *feel* a bit more of the pain and fear in Bobby. Right now I'm a little "outside" the action. Part of that is due to this passive construction: *Another shot was fired, but didn't hit him.* We need to be *in* Bobby's head. *He heard another crack. Asphalt splattered in front of him,* etc.

It's not enough to have an action opening. It's what the action feels like *to the character* that's essential.

You've got a potentially arresting hook here, but for it work to the max we need that POV "heat." Play the scene in your mind several times as if you were Bobby, then rewrite it.

Okay, so now you've got this guy being shot at, chased and then . . . flashback!

Ahhhh!

Don't do this. I know it feels like a little "teaser" but to the reader it's more like a "cheater." It's too obvious you're manipulating them by inserting a flashback to create an artificial cliffhanger.

So here's a rule of thumb: *No flashbacks in the first fifty pages.* When you put in a flashback too soon it stops the action cold and jars the reader. It pulls them right out of the fictive dream you've been weaving. (Note: I am not talking here about a "frame story," where we begin in the present then have the bulk of the book take place in the past. That's another matter entirely.)

Also, you're using an omniscient POV in the flashback. If Bobby *never even noticed* the young guy with the buzz cut, the only one who can see him is the author. This removes us further from Bobby. Keep the POV "hot" even in flashback scenes.

Now, what about flashbacks later in your fiction?

Remember, by definition they stop the action, so you'd better have a very good reason for using one (e.g., essential character background info that is so crucial you need to dramatize it).

And if you do use a flashback it needs to stand alone as a scene, with all the sensory description and intensity of a scene from the main plot line.

Flashbacks. Handle with care. But in the opening chapters, don't handle them at all.

Getting In and Out of Flashbacks

How do you get in and out of a flashback, so it flows naturally? Here's one way that works every time.

In the scene you're writing, when you're about to go to flashback, put in a strong, sensory detail that triggers the memory in the point-of-view character:

Wendy looked at the wall and saw an ugly, black spider making its way up toward a web where a fly was caught. Legs creeping, moving slowly toward its prey. The way Lester had moved on Wendy all those years ago.

She was sixteen and Lester was the big man on campus. "Hey," he called to her one day by the lockers. "You want to go see a movie?"

We are in the flashback. Write it out as a dramatic scene.

How do we get out of it?

By returning to the sensory detail (sight in this case) of the spider. The reader will remember the strong detail, and know that he's out of flashback.

Lester made his move in the back of the car. Wendy was helpless. It was all over in five minutes.

The spider was at the web now. Wendy felt waves of nausea as she watched it. But she could not look away.

Watch out for "had"

Watch out for the word *had* in your flashback scenes. Use one or two to get in, but once in, avoid them. Instead of:

Marvin had been good at basketball. He had tried out for the team, and the coach had said how good he was.

"I think I'll make you my starting point guard," Coach had told him right after try outs.

Marvin had been thrilled by that.

Do this:

Marvin had been good at basketball. [This gets us in. Now switch to scene] He tried out for the team, and the coach said how good he was.

"I think I'll make you my starting point guard," Coach told him right after tryouts.

Marvin was thrilled.

Flashback scene alternatives

An alternative to the flashback scene (which you may be tempted to turn into an information dump) is the *back flash.* These are short bursts in which you drop information about the past within a present moment scene. The two primary methods are *dialogue* and *thoughts.*

DIALOGUE

"Hey, don't I know you?"

"No."

"Yeah, yeah. You were in the newspapers, what, ten years ago? The kid who killed his parents in that cabin."

"You're wrong."

"Chester A. Arthur! You were named after the president. I remember that in the story."

Chester's troubled background has come out in a flash of dialogue. This is also a good way for shocking information from the past, or a dark secret, to be revealed at a tense moment in the story.

THOUGHTS

"Hey, don't I know you?"

"No." Did he? Did the guy recognize him? Would

everybody in town find out he was Chet Arthur, killer of parents?

"Yeah, yeah. You were in the newspapers, what, ten years ago?"

It was twelve years ago, and this guy had him pegged. Lousy press, saying he killed his parents because he was high on drugs. They didn't care about the abuse, did they? And this guy wouldn't, either.

We are in Chester's head for this one, as he reflects on his past. If you want to do a full flashback scene, thoughts can also operate as a transition point.

The skillful handling of flashback material is one mark of a good writer. Using back flashes as an alternative is usually the mark of a wise writer.

Listen to the Book

TCM, my favorite channel, showed a clip the other day of the great actor Eli Wallach talking about Method acting. This was the movement that took off in the 1940s, inspiring a new generation of actors like Brando, Newman and Dean.

Wallach reflected that as a young actor it was exhilarating to work things out with the Method. It was a like a big gymnasium and the actors were all playing off each other, trying things, letting scenes happen naturally.

But as he grew older, he said, he got more cautious. He

would sometimes forget those lessons of youth, that sense of play. To break out of his torpor he would reflect back on his early days.

"The Method tends to put you back on the track to enjoy what you're doing, to listen," he said. "The big secret to acting is listening. A thought on the screen is amazing. And if you really listen, it comes to life."

This hit me as something that applies to writing as well. We don't put our best words on paper unless, in some form or fashion, we listen to the story as it unfolds. Madeleine L'Engle put it this way: "A writer grimly controls his work to his peril. Slowly, slowly, I am learning to listen to the book, in the same way I listen to prayer. If the book tells me to do something completely unexpected, I heed it; the book is usually right."

So how do we listen to the book? Here are a few suggestions.

Listen in the morning

A valuable literary practice is to write quickly, first thing after you wake up (I will allow you a minute to start the coffee brewing, of course, but sit down ASAP and write, with pen and paper even, in stream of consciousness mode).

Dorothea Brande recommends this practice in her wonderful little book, *On Being a Writer*. It's a way to capture that netherworld we inhabit between sleeping and waking, and there is treasure there. Also, a lot of it you'll throw away. But that's the nature of creativity. The idea is to record as much of the mind stuff as possible, and then use whatever you find that's valuable. Like panning for gold, you get a whole bunch of the riverbed in your pan then coax out the gold a bit at a time.

Use a novel journal

Sue Grafton does this, and that's good enough for me. She begins each writing stint with her journal for that particular novel. She starts with a diary entry, something about her life at the moment. Then she starts asking herself questions about her WIP. She may want to work on a scene, or a character, or some potential clues, or whatever else is popping up in her mind.

Go to the place you fear

Going to the place we fear to go is often where the deepest and most vital material is found. My agent, colleague and friend, Donald Maass, is a master at helping writers press beyond safe pastures. A question Don likes to ask in his workshops is, "What is something your character would never ever do or say?" Then, find a place for the character do or say that thing. Or at least *think* it, showing a ferocious inner conflict. Wow. Try that some time and then pick up the pieces of your head.

If you ever get stuck on a project, or the inspiration for it has given way to drudgery, remember what Eli Wallach said. Maybe it's time to listen. Give the book your attention. Allow it to play. It wants to help!

Are you attentive to what your story is trying to tell you?

On Finding the "Premise" of Your Novel

A novelist's group I'm in was discussing the concept of the "premise" in fiction. It started with a book by Stanley D. Williams called *The Moral Premise,* which is aimed primarily at screenwriters.

The subject was familiar to me, as "premise" was first discussed (in my own experience) by Lajos Egri in his book, *The Art of Dramatic Writing.* A bit later another famous writing teacher, William Foster-Harris, defined fiction as a "problem in moral arithmetic" by which he was talking about the same thing.

Ditto for James N. Frey, in his two books, *How to Write a Damn Good Novel I & II.*

It is a way of describing the "point" of the novel, the "take away" value. Some might call it the theme. Formally, the premise is expressed (in Egri terms) like this:

Blind trust leads to destruction (*King Lear*)

Great love defies even death (*Romeo and Juliet*)

Frey states that every novel must have a premise. And only *one* premise.

For some writers this all seems complicated, but it doesn't

have to be. Confusion arises, I think, over how you "find" the premise. My own feeling that it's best "found" after you have set up the right conflict and characters.

Frey advises starting with characters who "demand to be whatever life you can create for them on the printed page. It is the characters who must galvanize you to write insisting that you tell their story."

In other words, if you have done your character and plot work up front, the premise will begin to reveal itself. Once you know the outcome you have, in Frey's words, the three C's — character, conflict and conclusion. And that will give you your premise. You can find this early in the novel, or later, but it'll be there somewhere.

Frey's process, then, is: Start with a character who grabs you, place him/her in a major conflict, and muse about the outcome.

Let's say you want to write a story about the Civil War. Well, you need a character to place in it. Maybe you pick a young Southern belle who has always gotten her way. Maybe you want to make it romancy, so you decide she's going to want to marry a certain Southern gentleman. Maybe you envision a handsome rogue will come along to complicate things. All that is floating around in your mind.

You start to sketch out this Southern belle, and she suddenly grabs you and you want to write about her. You decide the big conflict is going to be that her "true love" marries another, and she will have to scheme to get him some other way. And somewhere in there the Civil War breaks out.

You noodle on these possibilities, and then you think about a possible ending. Maybe she realizes at the end that she doesn't really love the Southern gentleman, but the rogue, and she and the rogue end up together, happy.

Meh.

You then think maybe this Southern belle has to suffer the consequences of her selfishness. She'll have married the rogue but realize too late that she really does love him. By then, her selfishness has driven him off.

This grabs you. You even think of a last line for the book: "Tomorrow will probably pretty much suck, too." (Later, your editor suggests you tweak that a bit.)

Anyway, you've now got the three C's. You can formulate a preliminary premise. If you just state it in your own words, it might be something like, "If you're selfish, and you keep on being selfish, you're going to end up alone. You're going to lose true love."

You can hone that down to an "officially sounding" premise if you like (e.g., "Selfishness in love leads to isolation") or simply leave it as is.

That much carries with it the opposite value, which you can define or not. The opposite would be, "Selflessness in love leads to lasting happiness" or something like that.

I think it's a good idea to go from the three C's to a premise statement slowly. Let the characters unfold the story awhile, because you may come across another premise you like better. Maybe your Civil War story was intended to be the "happy" ending . . . but as you wrote, you kept seeing your main character, Pansy, making all these selfish moves, and you decide a more memorable ending would be the "unhappy" one.

(Pansy, by the way, was the original name for Scarlett. I don't know when Ms. Mitchell made the change, but I am so glad she did).

This is a long way of saying to those of you who are flummoxed by the idea of a "moral premise," don't let it hound you. Write the three C's and put your heart into it. That will get you there eventually. Don't over think. William Foster-Harris put it this way: "Feel, don't reason, your way through a story!"

How to Write a Novella

One of our regular readers at the Kill Zone blog left a comment that said, "As a writer, it's been difficult to find information on writing novellas especially. Most articles I read say 'it's like a novel, only shorter.' Hello, Captain Obvious."

Well, if I may be so bold as to jump into a phone booth (wait, do they have those?) and emerge as Captain Craft-- as well as the author of currently selling novellas--let me take a stab at the subject.

Yes, a novella is obviously shorter than a novel. A rule of thumb puts the novella between 20,000 and 40,000 words.

The following are general guidelines for writing a novella. I say general because, like all writing tips, they are subject to change. But ONLY if you have a good reason for the exception!

1. One plot

The length of the novella dictates that it has one plot. It's a too short to support subplots. That doesn't mean you don't have *plot complications.* It's just that you are doing your dance around one story problem.

2. One POV

It's almost always best to stick with one point of view. For example, two of my novellas, *Watch Your Back* and *One More Lie*, are written in first person POV. That's because you want, in the short space you have, to create as intimate a relationship between the Lead character and the reader as possible.

As indicated earlier, more than one POV is acceptable *if you have a reason for including it.* And that reason is NOT so you can fill more pages.

A modern master of the novella is, of course, Stephen King. A look at his collection, *Different Seasons,* reveals three novellas written in first person POV. The exception is *Apt Pupil,* which is about an ex-Nazi's influence over a thirteen-year-old boy. The story thus has a reason for shifting between these two points of view. However, I note that *Apt Pupil* is the longest of these, and I actually suspect it's over 40,000 words, making it a short novel.

3. One central question

There is one story question per novella, usually in the form: Will X get Y?

In *Rita Hayworth and the Shawshank Redemption,* by Stephen King, the question is, will the wrongly convicted Andy Dufresne survive in God-awful Shawshank prison?

In *The Old Man and the Sea:* Will the old fisherman, Santiago, land the big fish?

A Christmas Carol: Will Ebenezer Scrooge get redemption?

4. One style and tone

There are novels that crack the style barrier in various ways, but a novella should stick to one tone, one style throughout.

In the old pulp days, novellas were common and usually written in the hard-boiled style.

My two novellas are done in the confessional style of James M. Cain--the narrator looking back at his past sins, detailing the consequences of same, with a twist ending.

Romance would have a different tone. Ditto paranormal. Whatever the genre, keep it consistent.

The Benefits of the Novella

Digital publishing has brought novellas back into favor. There are some story ideas that don't merit 90,000 words, but may be just right for 30,000. The suspense story is particularly apt for this form. One of the great masters, Cornell Woolrich, practically made his career on novellas of suspense.

An indie publishing writer can charge 99¢ to $2.99 for novellas. They can obviously be turned out more quickly than a full length novel.

Some Suggestions for Writing the Novella

1. Make sure your premise is rock solid

You don't want to travel down the road of a flabby idea, only to find out after 15,000 words that it isn't working. Come up with a premise that creates the greatest possible stress for the Lead character. For example, *One More Lie* is about a man accused of murdering his mistress. He's innocent of the crime, but guilty of the adultery. A bit of stress, I'd say.

2. Write in the heat of passion

Novellas are great for the NaNoWriMos among us. Getting the story down quickly releases that inner creativity we long for. And there won't be the need for as much revision as in a novel, which has subplot complications to deal with.

3. Use white space to designate scene changes

Instead of chapters, the novella usually employs white space between scenes. Some writers do break up a novella into sections designated by numbers. That's a matter of style. Just don't say "Chapter 1," etc.

4. Keep asking, How can it get worse?

Whether your novella is about the inner life of a character (as in *The Old Man and the Sea*) or the outer life of the plot (as in *Double Indemnity*), turn up the heat on the character as much as you can.

Think of the novella as a coil that gets tighter and tighter, until you release it at the end.

Some Famous Novellas

The Pearl, John Steinbeck

The Old Man and the Sea, Ernest Hemingway

A Christmas Carol, Charles Dickens

The Body, Stephen King

Double Indemnity, James M. Cain

A River Runs Through It, Norman Maclean

Phantom Lady, William Irish (aka Cornell Woolrich)

All Writers are Moral Philosophers

Some time ago I read Ayn Rand's writing reflections, *The Art of Fiction*. You may not know this, but she started as a screenwriter and playwright. This gave her an appreciation of structure, without which I don't know that her success as a novelist would have been possible.

Anyway, in talking about theme, which she emphasizes, she makes the point (rightly) that any story is going to have a worldview (she doesn't call it that), even one that seems to have no point . . . because that is a worldview, too. You can't escape leaving something for readers to ponder. The only question is how well you do it.

According to Rand, all novelists are, therefore, "moral philosophers." Some are just not very good philosophers (in that they haven't thought through their themes enough to know how to integrate them to the writing).

I like what she says about proving the theme through action. It's what the characters do, how they respond to or activate the plot, that proves the theme (or premise, as it is sometimes called).

Atlas Shrugged is 640,000 words long. And every word is there to support her premise, because she absolutely knew what it was.

Her editor, Bennett Cerf, made the mistake of suggesting a bit of editing to her.

"You vould not cut zee Bible, vould you?" she said.

The book was not cut.

It still sells tens of thousands of copies a year, over 50 years after publication.

So does *On the Road*, which was published that same year, 1957. In part, I believe, because every word of *that* novel supports Kerouac's premise that the point of life is the pursuit of "beatitude through experience." Kerouac knew the premise without articulating it as such, in a Randian way. But he was feeling it all the way through the writing.

You don't have to agree with the philosophy of a novel, Rand says, to appreciate the success or failure of the writer. She deems Sinclair Lewis a failure and Mickey Spillane a success.

Fascinating.

Referring to the section just before this one (the moral premise), combine these two ideas. Find your premise in the way that's most natural to you. Then, when you revise your novel, use that knowledge to deepen your thematic elements. You'll find lots of ways to do that, too. It'll make your rewrites all the more rewarding.

The Writing Life

Be Thankful That You're a Writer

I wrote the following post December 18, 2011, as my group blog, The Kill Zone, was going offline for a seasonal break. It seems to me a good post to review around holiday time, to reflect on the year past and the year to come, and to pause and be thankful for the blessings you enjoy. If there is one thing world religions and secular philosophy largely agree upon, it is that gratitude is the key to happiness. Learning how to be thankful consistently may take some practice and discipline, but it can be done. And it is so worth it.

You can start by being thankful that you're a writer.

Be thankful because you get to play. You get to make stuff up. You get to spin yarns that have the potential to *move* people. Do you know how hard that is to do? But when you do it, when you hear from a reader of your work who loved it—even if it's just your Uncle Harry—there's something magic in that transaction. And people today have precious little magic in their lives. You do.

So be thankful that you're a writer.

It's work, to be sure. It can be frustrating and bewildering and angering and insane. It can keep you up at night and wandering the streets talking to yourself like a mental patient without his meds (though what you are really doing is figuring out what your character might say in that scene you're working on). There are plenty of obstacles and setbacks that happen in a writing life, but you know what? Those are the very things that make you stronger. If you persevere, if you care, if you feel your calling in your heart and mind and sinews, if you know deep down that you're a writer, keep after it. If you do, when the dust all settles, you will have found a rich satisfaction in this passion of yours.

Because most folks don't feel much passion for anything. As Thoreau famously noted, the mass of people "lead lives of quiet desperation." But you're a writer, so at least if you ever *do* feel desperate, it's not going to be quiet! It'll shout and beat drums and cry and scream. But that very noise will pull you out of despair and get you back on the page, where your passion lives. Writing will save you from ever being stuck in the Land of Bland sequestered in the Army of the Drab.

In Herb Gardner's great play, *A Thousand Clowns,* Murray Burns tries to explain to his bland brother why he dropped out of the "rat race":

> **Arnold, five months ago I forgot what day it was. I'm on the subway on my way to work and I didn't know what day it was and it scared the hell out of me. I was sitting in the express looking out the window, watching the local stops go by in the dark, with an empty head and my arms folded, not feeling great and not feeling rotten. Just . . . not feeling. And for a minute I couldn't remember, I didn't know, unless I really concentrated, whether it was a Tuesday or a Thursday or . . . for a minute it could have been *any* day, Arnie. It scared the hell out of me. You got to know what day it is. You have to own your days and name them, each one of them, every one of them, or else the years go right by and none of them belong to you.**

You're a writer, and your days belong to you. You can name them and own them. Be thankful for that.

And don't fall into the trap of thinking money is the sole measure of success in this game. That's only a part of it. Even so, the incredible thing is that it's now more possible than ever for a writer to make *something* from writing. If you have the goods, you can find the buyers. The buyer might be a traditional publisher, or it might be a reader out there downloading digital. But you are living in a new golden age. Never have we had the choices we do now. Even if you only make a pittance it's within your power to do so, which means you're better off than the great majority of writers in the whole history of scribbling. Do you realize how fantastic that is?

Be thankful that you're a writer!

Don't be ashamed of it, don't be afraid to call yourself what you are, don't let the naysayers and critics (even if they are in your immediate family) keep you from doing what you love.

Here comes the new year. Resolve to write for all you're worth, which is inestimable. Because, as Brenda Ueland puts it, each one of you is original and talented and has something important to say. A writer is original, Ueland says, "if he tells the truth, if he speaks from himself. But it must be from his *true* self and not from the self he thinks he *should* be."

Be done with the *shoulds*. Tell your stories and don't hold back. Give your imagination freedom to run. Study the craft because it's your friend and helps you express your true self on the page.

And one thing more: Keep on writing for the rest of your life. Don't stop. Ever. Why should you? You're a writer, after all, and that's a wonderful thing to be.

Merry Christmas, Happy Holidays, and have a Joyous and Keyboard-Clacking New Year.

What Kind of Writer Do You Want to Be?

What makes a winner?

Is it going on a web cam and shouting *Winning?*

Is it having a lot of money?

Is it owning a lot of things?

Let me contrast a couple of writers for you. (These writers are composites, so don't ask me to name names.)

The first writer has had a couple dozen *New York Times* bestsellers in her career. She is not shy in saying she found a formula that sells a lot of books. And she keeps cranking them out, two or three a year now. Her publisher is very happy about this.

But her readers are beginning to feel like she's just "mailing it in." And in secret she'll tell you she can virtually sneeze out a book, and does. She spends a few hours a week writing and never edits her stuff. She just turns it in and lets the publisher do the rest. Which gives her plenty of time to travel to her chateau in Gstaad. Or to go to conference appearances, where she plays the diva in a way that even Joan Crawford would have applauded.

She has money. She owns things.

But is she a winner?

The other writer is someone you probably haven't heard of yet, but those who have read her books have not been able to forget them. While she writes in a certain genre, and is prolific, her novels never have a cranked out feel. That's because she cares about the writing too much. She cares about her readers too much. She could mail it in, but there's something inside her that makes her constitutionally incapable of putting out junk.

She doesn't have as much money as the first writer. Nor does she own as many things.

Is she a winner?

I'll tell you what, you can't get away from ancient wisdom. Buddha, Confucius, the Bible, the great philosophers . . . they have all been telling us that having money and owning things does not make you a winner. In fact, if you're not careful, they can shrivel you up into a thing that blows away like dried grass in a windstorm.

But this second writer, she can feel things the first writer no longer does (or perhaps never did). She feels the intense pleasure of working and caring and crying and laughing over her writing, of seeing things happen on the page that she *knows* are worth more than a million cranked out passages that exist just to earn more money so the author can own more things.

Is she a winner? Oh yes. And so is any writer in any genre who does more than just mail it in.

I'm talking about a writer who is courageous enough to have some skin in the game, and who isn't in this business just to make money and own things. If the money comes, that's great, that's awesome. We're not turning that down. But this kind of writer will never let it go to her head or her keyboard. She will refuse to do that to her readers.

In one of my favorite movies, *The Hustler,* Paul Newman plays Fast Eddie Felson, a pool hustler from Oakland who wants to be the best in the world. To do that he'll have to beat Minnesota Fats (Jackie Gleason), who hasn't lost a match in fifteen years.

At the beginning of the film Eddie does play Fats, and is winning. But some hubris on his part leads to carelessness. At this point Fats's manager, Bert Gordon (played with Faustian precision by George C. Scott), tells Fats, "Stay with this kid. He's a loser."

Well, Eddie does lose, and he's back to the bottom of the heap. In a bus station he meets a woman named Sarah (Piper Laurie), who is also at the bottom. She's pretty, but obviously has had a hard time of it. She drinks. She's been abused. Yet she and Eddie forge a relationship and he moves in with her.

One day he asks her, "Do you think I'm a loser?" He tells her about Bert Gordon's remark. Sarah asks if Gordon is a "winner." Eddie says, "Well, he owns things."

"Is that what makes a winner?" Sarah asks.

Then Eddie tells her how it feels to play pool. How anything can be great, even bricklaying, if a guy knows what he's doing and can pull it off. "When I'm goin', I mean when I'm really goin', I feel like a jockey must feel. He's sitting on his horse, he's got all that speed and that power underneath him, he's coming into the stretch, the pressure's on him, and he *knows.* He just *feels* when to let it go and how much. 'Cause he's got everything working for him--timing, touch. It's a great feeling, boy, it's a really great feeling when you're right and you know you're right. It's like all of a sudden I've got oil in my arm. The pool cue's part of me. You feel the roll of those balls and you don't have to look, you just know. You make shots nobody's ever made before. I can play that game the way nobody's ever played it before."

Sarah looks at him and says, "You're not a loser, Eddie, you're a winner. Some men never get to feel that way about anything."

What makes a winner? It's not money and it's not owning things. It's feeling *that way* about something.

Like your writing. Have you ever shed a tear over it? Have you got some skin in this game?

What kind of writer do you want to be?

[I wrote that on The Kill Zone blog, and it generated a number of comments. That provided me the opportunity for clarification on a couple of points. That is what follows.]

Re: *The Hustler*, I'm pleased you know the film. I hope more see it because of this post. An American classic. In my view, this isn't a film about self-worth. It's a film about a man who sells his soul to the devil for the chance to "win." It's Faustian. Rossen subtly makes that point when one of characters refers to a statue of the goat god Pan as resembling Bert Gordon. (The goat god was a stand in for the devil in medieval lit.) Eddie doesn't lack self-esteem (indeed, that's the one thing he has too much of) but a part of his own humanity. Alas, he finds it too late.

As he admits to Gordon at the end, he loved Sarah but "traded her in on a pool game." He tells Gordon that he was right about him, that talent wasn't enough. He had to have "character." That's what Eddie was missing. He admits now he found it, but only after that indecent in the hotel room in Louisville.

And he sees Gordon for who he is. "You don't know what winning is," Eddie said. "You're a loser, 'cause you're dead inside, and you can't live unless you make everything else dead around you." Eddie failed to see that what Sarah told him about being a winner was where he should have dwelt. He was already a winner and it wasn't a matter of money, or owning things.

As to winning being subjective, and a matter of contentment with just a material measure, I'm not sure I can agree with that, either. The ancient wisdom I refer to suggests otherwise. And when it comes to writing, I think there is a qualitative difference that emerges between the two composites that is worth noting.

Nothing here is illegal or immoral, of course. This is America, and you are allowed to make money. There's nothing really wrong in that. Cranked out dreck that doesn't hurt anyone, and is offered to the market for an exchange of dollars, has always been part of our economic system, whether we're talking books or Pet Rocks.

But maybe what I'd counsel to writers seeking to emulate

the first model is, be careful what you wish for.

****

I've not insulted anyone by calling them a "loser," even our first model. I've just asserted that this isn't the profile of a "winner," that money and owning things is not the sole measure. And here, the weight of history's wisdom is on my side. Can you name any great thinker who makes a persuasive case for the opposite? (Note: Ayn Rand might slip in through the back door, but she will be pretty much alone.)

Now, people who earn a living by "cranking out dreck" and are nice to their kids and dogs and neighbors, I have no quarrel with them. They are not "losers" and I would never slap that label on them. But that's really not the point of this post, which a second or third reading should make clear.

Also, I'm not at all sure about the "one man's trash is another man's treasure" idea. If so, any talk about quality in art is probably out the window. For example, if a crucifix in a jar of urine is "someone's treasure" I don't think the problem is merely subjective. But again, this is all rather tangential to my main point.

Let me say this again another way: I do not think that writing something entertaining, and doing it quickly, makes it "dreck." I believe in the value of entertainment. I have my own beliefs about how that should be delivered, and that informs my own writing. That's not what this is about.

What is Writing All About?

Some time ago I received a lovely handwritten letter from a high school student:

Dear Mr. Bell,

Thank you for your incredibly helpful books on fiction writing. "The Art of War for Writers" and "Revision and Self-Editing" have inspired me every time I open their pages. I first heard of you at a conference you held in Hilmar. I had an idea for a story at that time, and your "Art of War" book helped me realize what my idea could become. ~~After~~ During my busy years in High School this story has been on the verge of death several times. Your books full of helpful exercises and encouragement helped me keep my story alive, and I am incredibly grateful. Your writing style is very natural and always leaves me refreshed. Thank you again, a hundred times!

Sincerely,

How gratifying to actually get a letter (written on actual paper!) from a young lady who wants to write. She had come to a seminar I held in Central California, and apparently my books have helped her.

That, to me, is what writing is all about. If I had to pick one thing to explain why I do this, it would be that I want to move people with words. If it's fiction, I want to create an intense emotional experience. If it's non-fiction, I hope to instruct and entertain at the same time.

All other things—money, awards, "fame," professional associations—are ancillary to this, because those things come only *after* you connect with readers.

So that's why I do it, and getting letters or emails like this please me no end.

What about you? Take a couple of minutes and write out your answers to these questions:

1. Why do you write?

2. If you had to distill what writing is "all about" in a sentence, what would that be?

Let the answers simmer awhile, then revise them if need be. These will be your "guidance systems" as you continue your writing journey. It will help you remember to keep the main thing the main thing.

The Most Important Characteristic Every Writer Needs

There are three things that are required for success as a writer: talent, luck, discipline ... Discipline is the one that you have to focus on controlling, and you just have to hope and trust in the other two. —Michael Chabon

Talent is overrated. The ability to get tough, stick with it and produce words beats lazy literary giftedness every time.

That's where self-discipline comes in.

What every writer needs is their own inner drill sergeant. There are four things this sergeant needs to give you: motivation, action, assessment and time.

1. Motivation

Desire drives discipline. Mega bestselling writer Phyllis Whitney once said, "You must want it *enough*. Enough to take all the rejections, enough to pay the price of disappointment and discouragement while you are learning. Like any other artist you must learn your craft— then you can add all the genius you like."

You've got to go into this with the thought that nothing will stop you. And you've got to get yourself pumped up to do your work, which is *producing the words.*

One way to do this is with visual motivators. When I first started I got a coffee mug with WRITER written on it. I looked at it every day.

Another kind of visual is a "model of possibility." I found a picture of Stephen King that did that for me. It shows him working at home, his dog under his chair, his office stuffed with books and manuscripts, sitting back with his feet on the desk, editing a manuscript. That's what I wanted to be doing. I put this picture in a frame and set it in my office where I could see it every day.

Find your own visual motivators. Create some. It's not hard to do, and they'll get your blood flowing.

2. Action

The whole idea of motivation is to get you to take action. If you take action every day toward your goals you begin to feel unstoppable. Let's say you decide to write 300 words a day, 6 days a week. Maybe that's all you can manage because of your job or other life priorities. So you do it, and after a month you've acquired the habit. You keep this up and in a year you'll have a book. Keep that up over 20 years and you'll have 20 books, which is not a bad output at all.

If you have not set a weekly writing quota, do so now. What can you realistically accomplish in a week? I'll wait.

Good. Now, up that by 10%. Push yourself toward that goal each and every week.

3. Assessment

At various times, just like any business would, you need to step back and assess where you are and where you need to improve. At different stages of my career I would look at where I was in the craft and find weak spots. For example, a few books in I knew I'd become a good plotter, but decided my character work needed improvement. So I designed a self-study program. I gathered a bunch of novels with memorable characters and read them with an eye toward studying what the authors did. I took from my shelf of writing books those that dealt with characters and re-studied key sections. Every time I learned something I would write a scene using that tip or technique.

This needs to be systematic, something you do on a regular basis.

4. Time

Finally, you must learn to manage time. That's your real currency. When you are holding down a job or chasing kids around the house, finding writing time can be a challenge. But you can do it if you do three simple things:

a. Plan in advance (using Sunday to plan the week, with a calendar in front of you, is best)

b. Write it down (fill in your calendar with all your obligations, then block out times you can write)

c. Prioritize (learn to ignore those matters that are not important or urgent. Watching the Kardashians is not as important as finishing your novel)

The best book on the subject I ever read is now sadly out of print: *How to Get Control of Your Time and Your Life* by Alan Lakein (but you can pick up a used copy via Amazon's used book sellers. You can have one for under $5. Well worth it).

If you take seriously the above categories seriously, your odds of succeeding will go way, way up. There's an old sports saying: "Discipline beats talent where talent isn't disciplined."

It's true.

Class dismissed.

Don't Be Afraid to Fail Aggressively

I like Dwayne "The Rock" Johnson.

We all know he made his name as a wrestler, then got screen time as the Scorpion King because of the beefcake. Then he kicked it up a notch with *The Rundown* and *Walking Tall*.

But Johnson wanted to break out from just being the next action guy. He wanted to expand his range, into comedies. So he started working toward that end. People were skeptical. But in an interview with People magazine just before *Get Smart* came out, Johnson said, "I would rather fail being aggressive than being passive."

I loved that quote. I put it on a card and displayed it in my office. Because at the time, about three years ago, I was taking a big risk, too.

After over a decade in the fiction game I had a solid following in the Christian publishing world. My books hit the bestseller list and I'd won the top fiction award, the Christy. I could count on a certain number of readers every time out. I also liked the people and the companies I worked with.

But after twenty or so books, I wanted to stretch. The parameters of the inspirational fiction market are fairly well set. Plus, that market was trending toward a more "romance" feel, with a huge uptick in books depicting the Amish life. Now, I well understand the appeal of fiction that depicts simpler times and ways. I do not at all hold it against thee if thou likes Amish fiction.

But that's not my particular crevice in the fiction world.

So I had to make a decision. Stay put and play it safe? Or try something new and unproven?

Which is when I read the Dwayne Johnson quote. And I thought, If I don't try this now, I'll look back and regret it. It could end up being a ten-story dive into a glass of water, but Bugs Bunny did that, why can't I?

The worst that could happen was that I would "fail aggressively." There's no shame in that. It's what's driven all the innovations and breakthroughs in history. Edison failed more than he succeeded, but would never have succeeded at all if he hadn't been aggressive.

So I went and signed with Donald Maass, who showed great faith in my writing, and off we went. And the first thing that sold was my zombie legal thriller which is, I would say, a bit outside the box of my previous engagements!

Am I glad? Oh yeah.

As writers, we have to be willing to fail aggressively. If we don't, if we play it too safe, if we spend too much time worrying about the market and how to chase it down, we will lose that chance to be what the world prizes most — an original.

Sure, have some market sense, but put all that through the prism of your unique voice and vision and heart and desire. Then go for it. Don't be afraid of failure. You may be on the pathway to a breakthrough.

Listen to The Rock.

You Don't Have to be a Star

You don't have to be a star, baby, to be in my show. — Marilyn McCoo and Billy Davis, Jr.

Some years ago my lovely wife and I were in New York and went to see *Blithe Spirit* on Broadway. We had only one reason to go, the best in fact: Angela Lansbury. She's always been a fave of ours, and the chance to see her onstage (in, it turned out, her Tony Award winning role) was too much to pass up.

Sweetening the pot was that the male lead was Rupert Everett in his Broadway debut. It would be two "names" in a revival of a famous play.

When the curtain was about to go up an announcer told us that Mr. Everett would not be going on that night. His understudy would play the part. There were a few sighs of disappointment. Cindy and I comforted ourselves with the knowledge that the divine Angela, at least, was a go.

And she was stupendous. The production was a hoot.

And that understudy for Everett? He was *brilliant.*

So good that I looked him up on IMDB after the show. His name is Mark Capri.

Now, I was an actor for a time on the boards of the Big Apple, and appreciate a fine theatrical turn. Especially from a guy who the audience was initially disappointed to see (he won them over, however, and got huge applause at the end). So I wrote Mr. Capri a note to thank him for his performance.

I bring this up for writers because it illustrates a point. Mark Capri no doubt went into acting, as all thespians do, hoping to become a star. He did what actors are supposed to do. He got training (at no less than the Royal Academy of Dramatic Art in London). He was accepted into the Royal Shakespeare Company and began his theatrical apprenticeship.

Over the years he's played many roles in theatre (in a serendipitous touch, he made his New York debut with the same theatre company where I made mine, The Roundabout) and has had guest roles on TV.

In other words, he is a professional in every sense of the term. And when he was needed for that performance in *Blithe Spirit,* he delivered as a consummate pro should.

We are, as we all know, in the midst of the self-publishing revolution. More and more indie authors are making good money, not because they are "stars," but because they are professionals. The ones who think just tossing up mediocre material into the digi-system is going to make them rich are fooling themselves.

The ones who will make it will follow the same path as Mark Capri. They will train, they will get some good direction, they will write, they will keep writing. A miniscule number of them may even gain "star status," whatever that's going to look like in the future.

But I suspect the era of the superstar writer is coming to an end. The era of the solid professional is upon us. Those who learn how to do it all well (and I'm doing my part to help) will increasingly be able to realize the dream of doing something they love and making a living at it.

They will find their audience and please them with good performances. Just like Mr. Capri delivered that warm July night on Broadway.

Write Out Your Fantasy Writer's Bio

Here's mine:

JAMES SCOTT BELL was born August 10, 1912 in Arlington, Kansas. His father worked for the Chicago, Rock Island and Pacific Railways, but quit in 1918 and moved his family of ten to Tulsa, Oklahoma to work the oil fields. When Jim wasn't in school or working odd jobs, he was reading Zane Grey, Edgar Rice Burroughs and pulp magazines like *Black Mask.*

When the Depression hit, Jim rode the rails to Los Angeles and got a job as a cub reporter for the Hearst newspaper, *The Examiner.* By day, he tracked down stories of murder, fraud and corruption. By night, in his one-room apartment on Bunker Hill, he pounded out short stories for the detective magazines. He was published almost immediately alongside such luminaries as Horace McCoy, Erle Stanley Gardner and Dashiell Hammett. When his crime novella, *One More Lie,* hit the racks, Jim garnered instant national fame. The story sold to MGM and became the classic 1941 film starring Joan Crawford and Robert Taylor.

Jim became one of the most sought after screenwriters in Hollywood and contributed as much as anyone to the post World War II film noir genre. He continued to put out suspense stories for the paperback original market and pulp magazines.

In 1952, Jim and Robert Mitchum got into a fight with two henchman of mobster Mickey Cohen, who had been bothering a cigarette girl at the Brown Derby. One of the thugs pulled out a .38 and shot wildly, hitting Jim just above the heart. At the hospital Jim refused sedation and insisted that a studio secretary be summoned so he could dictate the final pages of a screenplay due the next day. That script went on to win an Academy Award.

Jim kept up his prodigious output of short stories, novellas, full length books and screenplays right up to his death at the age of 99. He had just typed *The End* on a novel when his heart gave out. His last words were, "Don't forget the mayonnaise."

Here is a picture of James Scott Bell in his office at Warner Bros. in 1947.

This flight of fancy is based on how I *feel* as a writer. I always admired the pros, the ones who could deliver the goods time after time. The writers who wrote to make a living and yet found a way to make their writing come alive.

What about you? If you could write your own writer biography, and it could be from any era, what would it look like? What sorts of books would you have written? Who would be in the movies based on your books?

This is not a mere game. Use this exercise to focus on your long term goals as a writer. Ask yourself how your imaginative bio might inform your writing today.

Go ahead. What are some of the entries in YOUR writer's biography?

Addendum on Pulp Fiction

What is pulp fiction anyway? Please don't get anywhere near confusing it with the nihilistic, over-praised and much too often over-copied film of the same name. True pulp fiction goes back to the magazines that used cheaper pulp paper in order to sell in great volume to a voracious reading public. These magazines had their heyday in the '20s, '30s and '40s.

It was fiction for the people, for the guy on the crowded subway going to work, or the busy mother with five kids who got a little reading time at night. It was for the people who wanted to be caught up in a fictive dream. It was not written in a style aimed at some elite literati. It was about dames and thugs and gats and roscoes. Femme fatales and corrupt police. About the American dream gone wrong and how crime does not pay. And it produced many superb writers along the way who transcended the genre.
Some stories became classics, in style and substance as well as plot. *The Maltese Falcon,* first serialized in the pulp magazine *Black Mask,* is a great American novel of any sort. It is what Shakespeare might have written had he been born in 1894 and walked the mean streets.

And how can you beat this opening by Raymond Chandler from his famous story, "Red Wind":

There was a desert wind blowing that night. It was one of those hot dry Santa Anas that come down through the mountain passes and curl your hair and make your nerves jump and your skin itch. On nights like that every booze party ends in a fight. Meek little wives feel the edge of the carving knife and study their husbands' necks.

I'm there. I'm seeing a slice (pun intended) of the human condition. At the time, Chandler was capturing a part of Los Angeles life that hadn't been given light before. He and another writer of the day, James M. Cain, were innovative in that.

But the thing I like most about pulp fiction is that it has to grab the reader and not let go. A storyteller with a "message" won't have a chance to deliver it unless he or she can make good on that basic, page-turning promise.

Pulp writers were prolific. They had to be at a penny a word. Quick story: Erle Stanley Gardner, like me an ex-lawyer looking to make a living as a writer, came up with the character Perry Mason. He got a penny a word at first, so in his stories you always see both names used whenever he describes a character. Like this:

Perry Mason entered his office and greeted his confidential secretary, Della Street, with a fond hello.

"It's about time," Della Street said.

"What's about time?" Perry Mason rejoindered taking a seat behind his desk.

Before Della Street could answer there was a quick knock and the door, and the private detective Paul Drake walked in.

"Hello, beautiful," Paul Drake said to Della Street.

You get the idea. Each time it was an extra penny earned! (You have to love how lawyers think, don't you?)

So this is why I write pulp fiction. I love to spin a good yarn and illuminate a little slice of the human soul along the way. The pulp market dried up, but now e-publishing has given it new life. It lets me be prolific, lets me keep testing new ways to grab readers, lets me keep doing what I've always wanted to do--write.

What Writers Can Learn from Tim Tebow

"There were ten guys in my writing class at Williams College who could write better than I. They didn't have what I have, which is guts. I was dedicated to writing, and nothing could stop me." —John Toland

In 2011 Tim Tebow was the talk of the sports nation. Unless you were collecting moon rocks at their place of origin, you read something about him during that time.

But just in case you were on Mare Tranquillitatis, let's summarize: Tim Tebow is the young quarterback of the

Denver Broncos who, in the 2011 season, pulled out miracle wins all over the place. This in spite of the fact that virtually all NFL prognosticators said he couldn't succeed in the league.

Yet, lo and behold, Tebow led the Broncos into the playoffs, and to their first playoff victory since 2005. And he did it in stunning fashion.

In a game against the vaunted Pittsburgh Steelers, big favorites to win, all Tim Tebow did was carve up the league's #1 pass defense for 316 yards. The last 80 of those yards will be celebrated forever in Bronco's history.

It was the first play of overtime. Tebow had played a great game, his best so far, but the Steelers had come back and tied it in regulation. Well, it took Tim Tebow all of 11 seconds to win the game in OT. He sold a fake run, got the Steeler linebackers to bite, then threw a strike to receiver Demaryius Thomas. Thomas caught the ball in stride, issued a sweet stiff-arm to Steeler defensive back Ike Taylor, and carried the rock all the way to the end zone for another miracle, magical finish.

I've been a Tebow fan since he played at Florida (which is a very hard thing for a USC Trojan to admit). What I love about the kid is that he harkens back to a time when athletes really did take role modeling seriously. Tebow, a devout Christian, does not act like an idiot off the field. He does not go to nightclubs with loaded firearms. He does not get hammered and sexually assault co-eds. He does not think, just because he has been blessed with amazing athletic talent, that he is immune from standards of civil conduct. He is, in short, what young men used to strive to be at one time in our society--a gentleman. (Even typing that sounds quaint nowadays, which does not reflect favorably upon "nowadays.")

But make no mistake. On the field Tim Tebow will cut your heart out. He will find ways to beat you. He will drive you crazy. Tebow, like all champions, is a fierce competitor in his arena of battle. I loved the shots of him on the sideline during the Pittsburgh contest. He had his game face on--intense, focused. And all this with the pressure of a lifetime on his shoulders.

You see, Tebow had played three mediocre to lousy games in a row. He was being counted out by the know-it-alls. He was a flash in the pan. He had no future in the NFL, let alone with the Broncos. So he not only had a playoff game to deal with, but possibly his whole future.

And yet he didn't fold, falter, or play scared. He took it right to Troy Polamalu and the fearsome Pittsburgh secondary and shredded them. (And yes, props to his coaches and teammates, of course. Tebow would be the first to point that out.)

So why do I bring this up for writers? Because we can learn something of the utmost importance from Mr. Timothy Richard Tebow. We can learn that it's not a matter of what other people say about you that counts. It's a matter of your heart and determination and guts. During his phase of getting criticized all over the place, Tebow never lashed out. He was full of humor and modesty.

Plus, he worked his butt off. He spent extra hours with his coaches, practicing his mechanics, giving every last ounce of energy to getting better at what he does.

The same should be true for you. You will get jeerers and critics in your writing life. You will endure negative comments and reviews and people — maybe even in your own family — telling you that you stink, or that you're deluding yourself with this writing thing.

Maybe you have the dream of being published by an established company. Perhaps you want to go it alone in the new world of digital self-publishing. Or some of both. Whatever your profile, if you care about writing, if it's a burning passion within you (I have nothing to say to those who are just out to make a buck), then you'll get your share of blowback, much of it unfair.

So are you going to let that stop you? Or are you going to keep working, keep typing, keep studying the craft?

In short, are you going to dig down and find a way to win?

The following game was against the New England Patriots. This one did not have a miracle finish for the Broncos. They were stomped, 45-10. Tebow was ineffective. But after the game he was gracious, answered reporters' questions, and said he was looking forward to the off season, where he intended to work hard to get better.

There is no "give up" in Tim Tebow. He will keep on finding ways to astonish us.

Go thou and do likewise.

No Fear, No Envy, No Meanness

Liam Clancy was one of the great Irish balladeers and a key figure in the folk renaissance of the early 1960s. Naturally he ran across 20-year-old Bob Dylan who was starting to get noticed in the coffee houses of Greenwich Village.

In the superb Martin Scorsese documentary, *No Direction Home,* Dylan recalls Clancy giving him some advice (fueled by more than a few pints of Guinness). "Remember Bobby," Clancy said, "No fear, no envy, no meanness."

That is a trinity of sound advice for writers, too.

NO FEAR

You have to go to new places, new depths, if you're going to be worth anything as a writer. Fear will keep you safe but it will never get you up the mountain.

Fear is not something we can always control. It's a feeling that sneaks up on you, and is actually healthy in certain situations. It can keep you out of a biker bar at midnight, for example. Not a bad thing.

But fear can also debilitate you and hold you back from your best work. Joan Didion said, "I write entirely to find out what I'm thinking, what I'm looking at, what I see and what it means. What I want and what I fear."

Go there. Write fearlessly. Let loose. Don't be afraid to "fail aggressively." (See the above entry.)

NO ENVY

Socrates called envy the "ulcer of the soul," and the wise old sage knew what he was talking about. Envy is a useless emotion that is, unfortunately, something most artists are prey to, even if they don't want to be. Suffice to say if you envy another's success you are only hurting yourself.

Besides, envy is baseless. The person you think "has it all" probably doesn't. I've known some bestselling authors who are miserable, to themselves and other people. A few are paranoid. Would I want to be them? Um, no.

Just work hard toward your goals and leave other people's success out of your equation. Practice gratitude. That is the key to happiness. I love what I do and what I have, my family and friends and career. I'm not going to poison that with pointless comparisons and petty thoughts.

Epicurus, one of the few Greek philosophers who got a whole school named after him, said, "Do not spoil what you have by desiring what you have not."

NO MEANNESS

Meanness in a writer is something I just don't understand. Most of the people I've met in the writing business are good, decent folks. I count many of them as among my closest friends in life.

But every now at then I run across a dyed-in-the-wool jerk. The diva. The narcissist. The sun around whom the rest of us are expected to orbit. I remember being at a book conference once when one of these exemplars was getting ready sign (as I was). But a sufficient supply of books was not at the booth, so this paragon of magnanimity started barking at the poor staffers, though they had several other tasks to attend to. The smile that was reserved for the public was gone, as was any hint of charity or appreciation.

It was all about this author, you see.

As author Michael Bishop once put it, "One may achieve remarkable writerly success while flunking all the major criteria for success as a human being. Try not to do that."

So there you have it. Simple, clear and solid advice from Liam Clancy, an Irishman who lived it: No fear, no envy, no meanness.

Try it. You'll be the happier for doing so.

Writers and Doubt

"Don't look back. Something may be gaining on you."— Satchel Paige

You want to be a writer? You *are* a writer? Welcome to the

world of doubt.

Dick Simon (of Simon & Schuster) once said, "All writers are scared to death. Some simply hide it better than others."

Why should that be? Even after one has reached the hallowed halls of publication? Even while in the midst of what might termed a career?

Because there is always lurking the idea that the rug may be snatched away. That some little dog will pull aside the curtain and reveal you there, a fraud after all. Even the top writers in the game get this feeling. No less a luminary than Stephen King cops to it.

Another reason excellent writers experience doubt is, ironically, excellence itself. Because these authors keep setting their standards higher, book after book, and know more about what they do each time out. That has them wondering if they can make it over the bar they have set. Many famous writers, unable to deal with this pressure, have gone into the bar itself, and stayed late.

Jack Bickham, a novelist who was even better known for his books on the craft, put it this way:
"All of us are scared: of looking dumb, of running out of ideas, of never selling our copy, of not getting noticed. We fiction writers make a business of being scared, and not just of looking dumb. Some of these fears may never go away, and we may just have to learn to live with them."

Yes, you learn to live with them, but how? The most

important way is simply to pound away at the keyboard.

You write.

As Dennis Palumbo, author of *Writing from the Inside Out*, put it, "Every hour you spend writing is an hour not spent fretting about your writing."

If a writer were to tell me he never has doubts, that he's just cocksure he's the Cheez Wiz of literature, I know I will not want to read his work. That's why I think doubts are a good sign. They show that you care about your writing and that you're not trying to skate along with an overinflated view of yourself.

The trick is not to let them keep you from producing the words.

Don't ever let the waves of doubt stop you. Body surf them back to shore, let the energy of them flow through your fingertips. That's the only real "secret" to this game.

How to Feel Miserable as a Writer

On her website, artist and writer Keri Smith generated a lot of blog noise with a list of ten ways an artist can feel miserable. I thought the list perfectly applicable to writers, and changed the wording slightly to reflect the writing life:

1. Constantly compare yourself to other writers.

2. Talk to your family about what you do and expect them to cheer you on.

3. Base the success of your entire career on one book.

4. Stick with what you know.

5. Undervalue your expertise.

6. Let money dictate what you do.

7. Bow to societal pressures.

8. Only do work that your family will love.

9. Do everything your editor asks you to do.

10. Set unachievable, overwhelming goals—to be accomplished by tomorrow.

You've Got to Please Yourself

But it's all right now,
I learned my lesson well.
You see, you can't please everyone,
so you
got to please yourself.

--"Garden Party" by Ricky Nelson

So, writer, do you write to please yourself? Do you write

for "the market"? Or is it something in between?

I advocate that you know about the market, have a sense of what's out there. This is, after all, a *business*. Publishers actually want to *make money*. Editors will talk about seeking fresh voices, but they also know they can be "too fresh" to sell to their pub boards.

But in the end, when you finally decide what story you're going to devote a significant chunk of time to, you've got to please yourself.

This is the pattern I followed for **Pay Me in Flesh**. I came up with a concept I thought was great for the market, something that hadn't been done before. Kensington took it on and I proceeded to write a book that pleased me — because that's the only way you can write something fresh and ultimately pleasing to readers.

That's my view, anyway.

Which brings me to Edna Ferber.

(What? How did he go from zombie legal thrillers to Edna Ferber? Watch!)

No one seems to read Edna Ferber much anymore. But in the early twentieth century there was scarcely a more famous, or more popular, American writer. From her first novel in 1911 to her last in 1958, she had one of the great careers in American letters. Not just novels, but plays (co-writing, among others, *Dinner at Eight* and *The Royal Family*), short stories, memoirs and newspaper columns.

I didn't know all this a year ago. All I knew about Miss Ferber (she never married) was that she wrote the novel for a film I've never been able to get into, *Giant* (1956). I find the movie overlong and mostly tedious. I'll watch some of it when it comes on TV for two reasons: a) to look at Elizabeth Taylor in her prime; and b) the final fight scene where an aging Bick Benedict (Rock Hudson) takes on a bigoted diner owner.

Anyway, one day last year I got a miserable head cold that had me whining around the house like a bored five-year-old. My wife finally told me to get out of her hair and into a sick bed. Too miserable to read, I turned on TCM to watch whatever was on.

It turned out to be a 1953 film called *So Big*, starring Jane Wyman and Sterling Hayden, both of whom I like. So I just started watching it and, what do you know? I got caught up in the sheer storytelling. It's about a Chicago girl who grows up wealthy, only to see her father lose everything. She's forced to take a teaching job in Dutch farm country.

It would seem like a recipe for a disappointing life. But Selina Peake is a woman of grit, with the ability to see beauty in the mundane. The practical Dutch don't get her at all, until she catches the eye of the big farmer, Pervis DeJong. They marry and have a son, and the story covers about thirty years after that.

I enjoyed the heck out of it.

The film was based on Edna Ferber's 1924 novel, which won the Pulitzer Prize. So I thought should read some

Ferber. I ordered a used copy of *So Big* and downloaded what's free from Project Gutenberg.

So Big was just as enjoyable as a novel. There is also an interesting afterword in my edition, a bit about Miss Ferber's life and craft. She started to get critical blowback the more popular she became. What a surprise. Some critics said she should have "written better" prose.

Edna Ferber's response is the reason I wrote this section and titled it as I did:

"Those critics or well-wishers who think that I could have written better than I have are flattering me. Always I have written at the top of my bent at that particular time. It may be that this or that, written five years later or one year earlier, or under different circumstances, might have been the better for it. But one writes as the opportunity and the material and the inclination shape themselves. This is certain: I never have written a line except to please myself. I never have written with an eye to what is called the public or the market or the trend or the editor or the reviewer. Good or bad, popular or unpopular, lasting or ephemeral, the words I have put down on paper were the best words I could summon at the time to express the things I wanted more than anything else to say."

You've simply got to please yourself.

The Comparison Trap

In addition to doubt, there's another mental obstacle that writers are heir to: the comparison trap.

It's almost automatic that we writers look at who is on the rungs above us and, in doing so, stay constantly anxious about our own position. Noxious things start popping into the mind: *Hey, I'm a better writer than he is. How come he's selling so much better than me? And what about that guy? He was nothing a few years ago when I taught at a conference. Where does he get off getting that advance? And then, of course, there's THAT one, the legend, the guy I admire most, the guy I wanted to be like, and it's pretty clear I'll never reach his level…*

And so it goes. A certain amount of this you might chalk up to the competitive urge, which is not, per se, unhealthy. We need a little of that warrior in us. But if you let it fester you'll be cooked. You'll start looking and acting like Ebenezer Scrooge in the first act of *A Christmas Carol.*

I thought of the comparison trap the other day when I read a story about American tennis star Andy Roddick. In 2001 this teenage phenom shot to #1 in the world after winning the U.S. Open. Here, it was assumed, was the next great superstar in the game, the new Connors, McEnroe, Agassi or Sampras.

There was just one problem, and his name was Roger Federer. The Swiss superstar came out of nowhere and proceeded to own Andy Roddick. They've met 22 times. Federer has won 20 of those matches. Federer has gone on to win a record 16 Grand Slam titles. Roddick is still looking for his second.

Roddick's best tennis may be behind him (aren't you glad your writing prime isn't based on athleticism?). He could look back and think that Federer's record might have been his.

But he's also accomplished more than most tennis players ever will. He's won several non-Slam titles, made it to #1 in the world, has a great Davis Cup record, he's rich and famous, married a model, and has a lifetime ahead as an ambassador for tennis. That doesn't exactly suck.

Here's something I tweeted that drew a lot of comments:

Comparison is death to a writer. Don't look up or down. Look at the page in front of you and nail it.

Every day I can look at another writer's career or recent success and get bent. Or I can be grateful for the career I have and keep doing what I do, which is write and try to do it better every time out.

There's something tremendously satisfying about that. I refuse to compare myself to others. Twenty years ago, unpublished, if I'd been shown my present career in a crystal ball I would have said Yes! Let me have that!

Gratitude is the great secret to happiness. Be content with what you have. You're unpublished? Be grateful you have the ability to learn the craft. Be grateful for new opportunities in the e-world. Your critique group getting you down? Be grateful for the people in your life who love you. Dogs and cats count, too.

And take a tip from Andy Roddick. "You keep moving forward until you decide to stop," he said recently. "At this point I've not decided to stop, so I'll keep moving forward."

Writers, Awards and The Journey

Of course, every writer--indeed, anybody who does anything--likes awards and recognition. That's our nature, and there's nothing wrong with it. Used rightly, it can be a motivation to good work and striving to get better.

But it should never be the dominating drive, in my view, or it will become a snare and a distraction.

One of my heroes is the late UCLA basketball coach, John Wooden. When I was in high school I got to attend his basketball camp, and talk to him a bit. Coach Wooden gave all of us a copy of his Pyramid of Success and taught us more than just the fundamentals of the game.

"Individual recognition, praise, can be a dangerous commodity," Coach Wooden once wrote. "It's best not to drink too deeply from a cup full of fame. It can be very intoxicating, and intoxicated people often do foolish things."

He was just as clear about losses. Never measure yourself

by what you lost, but by how you prepared. That's the only thing within your control and the only thing you can change.

"I never mentioned winning or victory to my players," Wooden said. "Instead I constantly urged them to strive for the self-satisfaction that *always* comes from knowing you did the best you could do to become the best of which you are capable."

That's his famous definition of success, and it's rock solid. When we work hard and know we've taken whatever talents we have and pushed them further along, that's achievement. It's one of the reasons I teach writing classes and workshops. I love helping writers get to their own next level, whatever it may be *for them.*

"I derived my greatest satisfaction out of the preparation, the journey," Wooden wrote. "Day after day, week after week, year after year. It was the journey I prized above all else."

In your own writing journey, don't getting distracted by the desire for recognition. Stay on the path, which is doing your best to write well every day.

*Quotations are from *Wooden: A Lifetime of Observations and Reflections On and Off the Court* by John Wooden and Steve Jamison (Contemporary Books, 1997)

The Rhino Skin Way

If you write for any length of time, especially professionally, you will come to know the inevitable bumps and potholes that dot the literary road. It may come in the form of a rejection letter, a bad review, an angry reader email, a personal jab from a family member, or any of a number of other slings and arrows.

This hazardous highway stretches from the moment you decide you want to write all the way to your grave marker. At the beginning stages, when you are unpublished, perhaps your Cousin Winifred remarks over the pearl onions at Thanksgiving, "You want to be what? A writer? You? How quaint. Pass the gravy."

Then, after you are published, the same cousin may aver, "They published *you*? Oh, well lots of people are getting published these days."

Cousin Winnie knows a lot of ways to get under your skin. Which is why you must begin to develop the skin of a rhino.
Rhino skin allows you to feel the hits but still get on with the important thing, the writing. All writers need such a coat.

So how do you get it?

1. Let it hurt for half an hour, no more

It's all right to take a hit and feel its full force. Don't try to hide the emotional impact. Give vent. Cry if you must. Hit a pillow. But let it all out in one burst. Action kills hurt. That leads us to #2.

2. Write

When my son fell off his two wheeler the first time out, I didn't let him quit. I got him back on the bike and almost burst my lungs running with him. We repeated the process till he got it.

He did not like falling. But when he was back on the bike and peddling, he was not thinking about the fall. He was thinking about staying up for the next few feet.

Writing is like that. When you are down about your writing, write. Dennis Palumbo, in his book *Writing From the Inside Out,* says "Every hour you spend writing is an hour spent not fretting about your writing."

Make a daily quota the tonic for your ache.

What you'll find is wonderful: when your mind snaps back to the hurt, it won't be as strong as it once was.

The more you do this, the more the hurt begins to fade. You won't forget it, but you won't be held back by it.

3. Vision

Return to your vision. Why do you write? Who do you want to be as a writer? What is it you want to say? What excites you?

A key to achievement is having in your mind a visual motivator, a picture of how it will feel to you when you reach your goal. Find that image and dwell on it.

4. Reward yourself

For a writing job finished, for a quota met, for a manuscript completed, heck, for just about anything, treat yourself to that indulgent dessert or movie night.

When I finish a manuscript I like to take a full day off and go on a literary goof. There are a few good used bookstores left in L.A., so I'll start there, browse the shelves, pick up that Cornell Woolrich I've been missing, or add to my collection of '50s paperback originals.

Then I'll go to a park and put out a chair and laze and read.

That night, I'll take my wife to one of our favorite places for dinner. Maybe a place in Malibu where we can watch the sun set over the Pacific. Or a pizza joint. It doesn't matter as long as we're together.

5. Remind yourself

Two reminders to put inside your head.

The first is to remember that the greatest writers of all time have been slammed in print. Many examples of this have been collected in a wonderful little book, *Rotten Reviews* by Bill Henderson. Here are a couple of my favorites.

Thomas Bailey Aldrich, writing in the *Atlantic Monthly* in 1892, said of Emily Dickenson, "An eccentric, dreamy, half-educated recluse in an out-of-the-way New England village — or anywhere else — cannot with impunity set at defiance the laws of gravitation and grammar. Oblivion lingers in the immediate neighborhood."

Nothing of Mr. Aldrich, to my knowledge, remains in print.

The eminent Clifton Fadiman, in *The New Yorker* no less, said of Faulkner's *Absalom, Absalom!* that it was "the final blowup of what was once a remarkable, if minor, talent."

When you get a bad review or comment, remember you're in very good company.

And then remind yourself *constantly* that you are a writer, because you write. There are many more people who do not write yet feel perfectly at ease sniping at those who do. When such a snipe comes your way, remind yourself that you are the one putting yourself on the line, opening a vein, walking the tightrope, singing a solo under hot lights. You are part of a courageous bunch who are all about *doing*. Teddy Roosevelt's famous advice applies to writers:

"It is not the critic who counts: not the man who points out how the strong man stumbles or where the doer of deeds could have done better. The credit belongs to the man who is actually in the arena, whose face is marred by dust and sweat and blood, who strives valiantly, who errs and comes up short again and again, because there is

no effort without error or shortcoming, but who knows the great enthusiasms, the great devotions, who spends himself for a worthy cause; who, at the best, knows, in the end, the triumph of high achievement, and who, at the worst, if he fails, at least he fails while daring greatly, so that his place shall never be with those cold and timid souls who knew neither victory nor defeat."

Get in the arena. Go at your writing with all the devotion and love and enthusiasm you have. When darts come your way, keep writing. You will grow Rhino skin.

My Top 10 Writing Influences

A common interview question for writers is, Who were your literary influences? I've given it some thought over the years and have come up with a list of my top ten. Here they are, in no particular order:

Franklin W. Dixon

This was, of course, the cover name for the Hardy Boys series. Several authors did the actual work (a Canadian named Leslie McFarlane was the first). From *The Hardy Boys* I learned that you could make readers read on by ending a chapter with an exclamation point! Today I don't use the actual punctuation mark, but try to achieve the same feeling—so readers have to turn the page.

The Classics Illustrated comic books guys

I loved the old Classics Illustrated series. I got acquainted with much great literature that way. *The Hunchback of Notre Dame, The Count of Monte Cristo, The Adventures of Robin Hood, Men of Iron* and on and on. Beautifully illustrated and written. I learned pure storytelling from these little gems.

Edgar Rice Burroughs

My first "grown up" novel was *Tarzan of the Apes.* I loved the experience of being pulled into a big story and then not wanting it to end.

William Saroyan

My beloved high school creative writing teacher, Mrs. Marjorie Bruce, encouraged me to read more than sports biographies. At a book fair she got me to buy *My Name is Aram,* which is still one of my favorite collections of short stories. I love Saroyan's whimsical voice.

Ernest Hemingway

In college, Hemingway knocked me out. I think he is the greatest short story writer who ever lived. His style is easy to satirize, but no one has ever been able to do it better — not even the lionized "minimalists" of current fashion. I am very proud to have been a semi-finalist one year in the Imitation Hemingway Contest.

Jack Kerouac

I think most college guys who are into literature go through a Kerouac phase. I ate up *On the Road* and Kerouac's idea of "be-bop prose rhapsody." Even now I try to follow some of his writing techniques, like:

– Submissive to everything, open, listening

– No time for poetry but exactly what is

– Believe in the holy contour of life

Raymond Chandler

Oh man, when I discovered Chandler, I was in heaven. Still the best prose stylist of any hard-boiled school you want to name. Nothing more needs to be said.

John D. MacDonald

Storyteller supreme. Great stylist of "unobtrusive poetry." I'm thinking mainly of his '50s stand-alone novels. The Travis McGees are enjoyable on their own and have much to commend them. But his output before that was amazing and the top quality of the paperback writers of the day.

Dean Koontz

I learned a lot from Koontz about how to write a flat-out page turner. Koontz also wrote a superb book on the craft, *How to Write Bestselling Fiction*. It's out of print and goes for about $200 on the open market. I got mine off a library giveaway shelf and still refer to it.

Stephen King

King puts it all together. A great stylist, plotter and character creator. I read King and sometimes just shake my head at how good he is. Please don't bring up the fact that he also sometimes seems to be the king of F-bombs. He succeeds in spite of, not because of, that little fact.

Who are your writing influences? A good exercise would be to make a list like mine, then go back and look at the works of your favorite authors. What is it there that grips you? How can you create that in your own writing?

Give it some thought. This is the road to getting better.

Type Hard, Type Fast

I believe in fast writing.

Fast writing does not mean hack work (it can, of course, but it's not necessary). In fact, writing faster helps noodle the creative imagination and gets to material we might otherwise miss.

Concentrated effort is what I'm talking about. This means great work can be done relatively quickly, and not only by "geniuses." Further, I contend that many young writers would actually improve their craft—and chances of getting published—if they would write faster, especially at the beginning of their learning curve.

First, a few facts. Some of the best novels of the past century were produced at a rapid clip by authors who found writing time each day, and simply went at their task with singular resolution:

– William Faulkner wrote *As I Lay Dying* in six weeks, writing from midnight to 4 a.m., then sending it off to the publisher without changing a word.

– Ernest Hemingway wrote what some consider his best novel, *The Sun Also Rises*, also in six weeks, part of it in Madrid, and the last of it in Paris, in 1925.

– John D. MacDonald is now hailed as one of the best writers of the '50s and '60s. Within one stunning stretch (1953-1954) he brought out seven novels, at least two of them — *The Neon Jungle* and *Cancel All Our Vows* — brilliant (the others were merely splendid). Over the course of the decade he wrote many more excellent and bestselling novels, including the classic *The End of the Night*, which some mention in the same breath as Truman Capote's *In Cold Blood*. Also *Cry Hard, Cry Fast*, which is the basis for the title of this blog entry.

So prolific was MacDonald that he was needled by a fellow writer who, over martinis, sniffed that John should slow down, ignore "paperback drivel" and get to "a real novel." John sniffed back that in 30 days he could write a novel that would be published in hardback, serialized in the magazines, selected by a book club and turned into a movie. The other writer laughed and bet him $50 that he couldn't.

John went home and, in a month, wrote *The Executioners*. It was published in hardback by Simon & Schuster, serialized in a magazine, selected by a book club, and turned into the movie *Cape Fear*. Twice.

– Ray Bradbury famously wrote his classic *Fahrenheit 451* in nine days, on a rented typewriter. "I had a newborn child at home," he recalls, "and the house was loud with her cries of exaltation at being alive. I had no money for an office, and while wandering around UCLA I heard typing from the basement of Powell Library. I went to investigate and found a room with 12 typewriters that could be rented for 10 cents a half hour. So, exhilarated, I got a bag of dimes and settled into the room, and in nine days I spent $9.80 and wrote my story; in other words, it was a dime novel."

– Jack London was anything but promising as a young writer. He could hardly string sentences together in a rudimentary fashion. About all he had was desire. A burning desire. So he shut himself up in a room and wrote. Daily. Sometimes 18 hours a day. He sent stories off that got returned. He filled up a trunk with rejections. But all the time he was learning, learning. When he died at the age of 40 he was one of the most prolific and successful writers of all time.

– John O'Hara wrote fast, and well, turning out books, stories and plays over the course of his long career.

– Charles Dickens wrote fast. He had to. He had ten

children. And he wrote many of his novels in installments for literary magazines. He had to keep the chapters coming.

– But even Dickens pales when compared to Anthony Trollope, author of some 47 novels (thrice the number Dickens wrote). Yet Trollope wrote a good many of these while working full time as a civil servant.

How did he do it? He produced a quota of words every day. If he got to the end of a novel and hadn't reached his daily quota, he pulled out a fresh sheet of paper, wrote "Chapter 1" on it and kept going.

– Stephen King says he used to write 1500 words a day, every day, except his birthday and the 4th of July. A prodigious output — and the prestigious National Book Foundation Award for Distinguished Contribution to Literature — are the result of this steady pace.

One could go on, but the lesson is clear. Writing "genius," like any other kind, is 99% perspiration. These authors all worked extremely hard early in their careers to learn their craft. By writing fast they virtually forced themselves to learn. Their books were not the product of small bits of inspiration, but rather steady, dedicated, intense work, day after day.

Now, I think many young novelists would do well to write faster. First, you learn most about writing a full length novel by actually writing a full length novel. It is much more valuable to do this repeatedly than to hover too long over one unfinished (or unpolished) manuscript.

Second, you become a professional in the best sense of the word (well, maybe second best, after getting paid). A professional is someone who does his job, every day, even if he doesn't feel like it. A surgeon can't refuse to operate because he's upset over the Dodger game last night. A criminal defense lawyer can't ask for a continuance so he can go to the beach and dream of someday getting a client who is actually innocent.

And a professional writer can't sit at the computer playing Spider Solitaire, waiting for a visit from the Muse. A pro is someone who writes, whether inspired or not, and keeps on writing.

I've counseled many writers at conferences who have come with a single manuscript yet haven't got another project going. I tell them, "That's wonderful. You've written a novel. That's a great accomplishment. Now, get to work on the next one. And as you're writing that next one, be developing an idea for the project after that."

You see, publishers and agents are not looking for a book. They are looking for solid, dependable writers. They invest in careers. They want to know you can do this over and over again.

The best advice I ever got as a young writer was to write a quota of words on a regular basis. I break my commitment into week-long segments (anticipating those days when I ride a bike into a tree or some such). I believe this discipline has made all the difference in my career. The testimony of so many other professional writers attests to its value.

One such testimonial comes from Isaac Asimov, author/editor of 500+ books. He was once asked what he would do if were told he had only six months to live.

"Type faster," he said.

Muzzle of a Deadline

I love deadlines. I like the whooshing sound they make as they fly by. — Douglas Adams

My friend, thriller writer John Gilstrap, once tweeted this: "Staring down the muzzle of a deadline, I'm beginning to panic."

All of us who write under contract know that feeling. At the time of this writing I'm on deadline for two books, one fiction and one non-fiction. Through some inscrutable machination of Murphy's Law (or as a punishment from God) both manuscripts are due about the same time. Add to that galley proofs that I have to get done by next week, and you have a prescription for rubber room admittance. I find myself walking around the house with my hand in my shirt, crying "Josephine! Josephine!"

My author colleagues know what I'm talking about.

But if you backed us up against the wall at a party, and forced us to elaborate further, we'd probably admit there's a certain "high" in staring down that muzzle. Our nerve endings are on edge, we know deep inside that's motivation to get cranking, that we're on full alert, all our senses at the ready, like a hunter who knows the lion (if I may be Hemingway-esque for a moment) is silently watching from the bush.

Does that make any sense? Or shall we just accept the fact that the writing life is a strange hybrid of joy and misery which, when mixed together, intoxicates with a seductive allure?

For those of you still awaiting publication, this is what you're in for.

And while you are waiting, may I suggest you train yourselves now and create your own muzzles?

First, finish your book. Finish it! Give yourself a completion date. There are many reasons people have for not completing a book, most of them bad. Fear of failure might be one. Fear of hard work another (it's fun to keep creating, less so get critiqued and fix things).

But you learn so much from completing a novel it's best to do it as fast as you comfortably can.

Which brings us to the quota. I know there are some writers who reject the idea of a consistent production of words. But most, I think, see the absolute value of it.

This was one of the earliest pieces of advice I got, and helped me at just the right time in my career. It's also allowed me to see published 25 books in a little over 15 years. Not a bad output. In fact, I look back with some astonishment at the record, and owe it to the quota.

I know there are other authors much more prolific than I, but I found just the right number to please my desire for production and my standards for the craft. I'm right where I want to be.

My suggestion is that you set a weekly quota. This is so you can break it down into days, and should you miss a day (which you will) you can make it up on the others.

Anthony Trollope was working for the British postal service and trying to become accepted as a novelist, when he began a quota system for is writing. In his autobiography he wrote:

There was no day on which it was my positive duty to write for the publishers, as it was my duty to write reports for the Post Office. I was free to be idle if I pleased. But as I had made up my mind it to undertake this second profession I found it to be expedient to bind myself by certain self-imposed laws. When I have commenced a new book, I have always prepared a diary, divided into weeks, and carried it on for the period which I have allowed myself for the completion of the work. In this I have entered, day by day, the number of pages I have written, so that if, at any time, I have slipped into idleness for a day or two, the record of that idleness has been there, staring me in the face and demanding of me increased labor so that the deficiency might be supplied.

You want to make it in this racket, you produce the words. You don't need the muzzle of a contract deadline to do it. You can set your own.

Now if you'll excuse me, I have to go correct some pages.

Josephine!

Find Your Inner Erle Stanley Gardner

Somewhere inside me lurks the shadow of Erle Stanley Gardner.

Gardner, of course, wrote the Perry Mason series. He was at one time, right up into the 1960s, the world's best-selling writer. It was a testimony to two things. First, his dogged determination. He wrote something like a million words a year for several years before he broke out. Second, he became a master of the essentials of entertaining fiction: a Lead character you cared about and plots that tested him to the limit. Perry always got the seemingly impossible case, and Hamilton Burger was certain this would be the one where he would clean Perry's clock.

Not so. Perry always found a way to win, using his inductive and deductive powers as well as his in-court technique. And readers lapped it up.

Gardner was prolific. At least a million words per year.

We are in a new day now with e-book publishing and that is a boon to writers who like to entertain and have more stories to tell than can be published in print form. My first straight-to-e-book, *Watch Your Back,* is a novella and three stories. The e-book format is the only way it would appear.

And so it has. There will be more.

I like the feeling that we're back in those days when Gardner pumped out stories and pulp magazines published them. And then his novels, too.

Learn from Gardner. To make it as a writer requires a strong work ethic and a continuing learning curve.

When you write, write. Don't be thinking about trying to make it perfect the first time.

When you finish a draft, look at what you've written and figure out how to make it better. You can read books and magazines on writing, get critiques, go to conferences. Keep writing all the way through those things.

If you do those things — learn and write, write and learn — and never stop, you have a chance to do well as a writer. Old Calvin Coolidge, not the most quotable of Presidents, once said, "Persistence alone is omnipotent."

Prove him right.

Doing the Asimov

Writers are nuts. Crazy. Not right in the head.

You have to be, at least a little bit. I mean, you want to make stuff up and expect to get paid for it? You want people to give you money for lying? You could go to law school for that. Why write?

You want to invest years of time plugging away at fiction with no guarantee of return? You want to endure the looks of pity and scorn you get around the Thanksgiving table when it's your turn to talk about what you do?

Yes, we're all more than a little nutty in this game.

Sometimes, it gets even crazier. Like now.

I'm doing "The Asimov."

Isaac Asimov was one of the most prolific authors of all time. Something north of 500 books. Not just fiction, but science, history, biblical studies, jokes. Sheesh, how did he do it?

By having no life, that's how (he said so himself). Asimov had several typewriters around his New York apartment, each with a different project in it. When he tired of working on one he got up, stretched, walked across the room and went to work on another.

He'd "snatch time." If he had a fifteen minute wait for something—say, guests to arrive—he'd write.

A divine madness, that's what possessed him. And I fully understand it.

I've been working all morning on edits of a manuscript, brainstorming new scenes for a novel in progress, reading pages for two projects on which I'm a consultant, hammering out final details on my seminar. Then I looked at the clock. I thought an hour had gone by. But it was lunchtime.

I made myself a steak sandwich, then parked in front of the TV to watch a little ESPN while I ate.

I also grabbed my AlphaSmart Neo, the nifty, light, dedicated word processor that runs on AA batteries, upon which I am now typing this essay.

Type. Eat. Watch. Stupid Dodger owner. Type. Eat.

Cut to:

The steak sandwich is gone. And I've got a book section almost done.

That's The Asimov.

I have some writer friends who say they cannot do this. They can only concentrate on one project at a time. Personally, I think they'd find The Asimov refreshing. Taking a "rest" on one project lets the brain cells work on it under the radar.

But who knows? Brains are wired differently. That's why we have *Jersey Shore* and *Masterpiece Theater* coming out of the same box.

What about you? Can you work on more than one project at a time, with the same intensity? Why not give it a try?

1. Plan it out. Pick three or four projects to concentrate on.

2. Make one project your primary. That should be a novel in progress. Have one going at all times.

3. Write in short spurts, maybe 25 minutes at a time. Take a 5 or 10 minute break, then write on another project. See how this works for you.

4. Snatch time. Be ready to a little typing or writing when you've got a free moment.

You may like The Asimov. Give it a whirl and see.

Now if you'll excuse me, it's time for some ice cream.

Finding a Mentor

Every writer needs a mentor. Or at least someone to offer encouraging words during those dark, dismal days of doubt (like when you use too much alliteration and wonder if you'll ever get this writing thing right).

Many writers had an English teacher or creative writing instructor in school who gave them encouragement. I had the good fortune of taking creative writing from Mrs. Marjorie Bruce at good old Taft High. She saw something in me when all I saw was a jock who wanted to play college hoops. She really got me going and believing in myself as a writer, and I kept in touch with her for the rest of her life, until she passed into that great classroom in the sky at the age of 90.

I went to college where they undid some of Mrs. Bruce's good work. There I was told: *Writers are born, not made. You can't really learn this stuff. You either have it or you don't.* And I certainly didn't have it. I thought writers just sat down and plots and great characters burst out of their fingertips without any effort whatsoever. And I couldn't do that.

So life went on, I did other things, got married, went to law school. But one day I woke up and realized I still wanted to write, that the desire had never gone away. So I set out to try to learn what they said couldn't be learned.

And one of the first people I found who helped me along was Lawrence Block. I read his book, *Writing the Novel,* and knew at last I had found the encouraging mentor I was looking for. I subscribed to *Writer's Digest* and read Larry's fiction column every month. I still have big binders on my shelf full of old copies of the magazine, with his columns copiously underlined.

He seemed so able to communicate what it *feels* like to be a writer, and how a writer thinks. I never read any column of his where I didn't nod my head at least a couple of times, thinking here is a guy who really gets it. And he's generous enough to give it to others.

But it wasn't just his instruction, it was his fiction. The first novel of his I read was *Eight Million Ways to Die*. It blew me away. I consider it one of the classics of the crime genre. It motivated me. I wanted to be able to write a book someday that packed that kind of punch.

Years later, when I was offered the fiction column at *Writer's Digest*, I felt like some junior prophet who was taking over the sacred page from Moses. It was a privilege, and I tried my best every month to give readers what Larry had given me.

Search for someone who writes about the craft in a way that resonates with you. Go back to those books time and again when you need an extra push.

And here's a little writing trick: When you're stuck in a portion of your story, or have some doubts about it, imagine your mentor (or favorite writer) standing beside you, and hear what he or she has to say about the work in progress. That little "opening up" of your imagination might give you the very tip you need to press on.

Writer Quotes at Starbucks

I collect quotes from writers on all aspects of the writing life. They open up little windows in my mind and help me see things I might miss on my own. I like to review these quotes from time to time. It makes me feel I'm in on a big conversation about my profession, with a bunch of very cool and experienced people. The only thing missing is the Starbucks.

Actually not, as I'm typing this right now at my favorite table at my favorite Starbucks. I'll just pretend it was Ray

Bradbury who bought me that first cup, as he sits down with me and says,

"I do a first draft as passionately and as quickly as I can. I believe a story is only valid when it is immediate and passionate, when it dances out of your subconscious. If you interfere in any way, you destroy it . . . Let your characters have their way. Let your secret life be lived. Then at your leisure, in the succeeding weeks, months or years, you let the story cool off and then, instead of rewriting, you RELIVE IT. If you try to rewrite, which is a cold exercise, you'll wind up with all kinds of Band-Aids on your story, which people can see."

Thanks, Ray. When I read your work that's exactly the impression I get, that your incredible imagination has been frolicking around in the fields and having fun. And by the way, thank you for *The Illustrated Man*, which was one of those life-changing books for me. When I read it in junior high, I thought, man, to be able to write that way someday...

Ah, I see that Henry David Thoreau, looking awfully good for a dead guy, has joined us. First thing out of his mouth is,

"How vain it is to sit down to write when you have not stood up to live."

Right on, Hank. If there's nothing of value inside the writer, how can there be anything of value for the reader? And you can't buy value, like vowels on *Wheel of Fortune*. You have to earn it by living. Reminds me of something I heard once, that a writer really doesn't have much to write about until he's 40. That may be a bit high, but there's something to it, I think. Live first, write second.

Here's Barnaby Conrad, the man who started the famous Santa Barbara Writers Conference, and a terrific writer himself. As he drags a chair over, he says,

"Remember, almost no writer had it easy when starting out. If they did, everyone would be a bestselling author. The ones who make it are the stubborn, persistent people who develop a thick skin, defy the rejection, and keep the material out there, trolling."

Boy, is that ever true, Barnaby. When I wrote my first screenplay, I thought it was a work of pure, natural genius. The first industry friend who read it said, "You don't have it." I first thought she meant I didn't have any talent (as some of my former criminal clients have averred). But she explained I didn't have it ON THE PAGE. I realized I had a big learning curve ahead of me.

I wrote six full length screenplays over the next two years or so, before I landed with a Hollywood agent and began getting anywhere. Before that, I almost broke a knuckle knocking on doors and getting them slammed in my puss. Which is why Andre Dubus, who has brought his latte to our table, interjects,

"Don't quit. It's very easy to quit during the first ten years."

That catches the ear of the ghost hanging out with Thoreau, George Bernau, who wrote *Promises to Keep* and other novels. He was a practicing attorney when he got into a car accident and almost died. In the hospital he took stock of his life, and, as he reminds us,

"I decided that I would continue to write as long as I lived, even if I never sold one thing, because that was what I wanted out of my life."

If you have the desire to write, then make the decision now that you'll write—strongly, passionately, with a commitment to your craft—no matter what.

When I Get the Writing Heebie Jeebies

heebie-jeebies | hēbē jēbēz |, pl. n., *a state of nervous fear or anxiety*

I love virtually everything about writing fiction.

Getting the idea is the most fun. I can come up with concepts all day long. Ideas constantly pop into my head, or I'll see something on the street that gets me asking, "What if . . . ?" I write these down put them in an electronic file. Every so often I go over the ideas and cut-and-paste the best ones into a document called "Front Burner Concepts."

Eventually one of these grabs hold and says, "I'm the one, Dude." And then I'm totally jazzed. Because starting a book with a killer idea is like falling in love. The writing of a first draft is like the first year of marriage. You're committed. You've still got glow. It's young love and that keeps you going, keeps you bringing flowers to the project all the way through.

Then comes the editing process. This is like marriage counseling. Now you've got to work to keep you and your story together. There are problems to address. And if you've received an advance, divorce is out of the question. But with time and patience and some give-and-take, you've got your final draft done.

And then...

I get the page proofs from my publisher. This is where I get the heebie jeebies. This is the last time I'll get a crack at the book before it goes to the bookstores and readers.

Which is why I never read any of my books once they're in print. I'm too afraid I'll find a mistake, or something I wish I'd phrased differently. At least with digital self-publishing one can make changes fairly easily. But in the traditional world, usually it's one-and-out.

Keep this in mind, no matter how you publish. It's not all fun and games. There is hard work along the way and more than a few tremors. But it's worth it!

Social Media Marketing Made Easy

Shortly after the launch of my e-books I started getting emails from author friends, some of whom are flummoxed or annoyed about the whole social media marketing thing. These are established writers, too, who feel under pressure to Tweet this and Face-book that, and blog the other thing. All of which takes time away from what they want to do most — write fiction.

And then there are the newbies, who are being told *You have to have a platform* even before you have a book, which always seems like telling a Sea Scout he has to build a boat before he can go to the beach.

It's a real concern, because too much stress and attention put on self-promotion and marketing can actually have an adverse affect on your writing, and even your personal life. On the other hand, an author does need to get in the game in *some* way.

So what's the balance? What follows are some tips for getting a foothold in social media marketing. They seem to work for me, so do with them what you will.

1. Specialize

Don't try to be active on every possible platform. You'll end up diluting your effectiveness in each. Instead, choose two or three and get really good at it.

For me, it's primarily blogging (at The Kill Zone) and Twitter. I find the substance of blogging once a week, and the real time of Twitter each day, the perfect blend. On occasion I drop into other blogs and comment if I feel I have something to add to the discussion. I do have a Facebook author page.

I do an occasional video about writing.

The smartest social media guy I know, Thomas Umstattd of Author Tech Tips, says, "It is much better to specialize. Seth Godin does not do Twitter or Facebook. He just has the most popular blog ever. Be faithful in a few areas and then you will be ready to be faithful in many areas."

2. Don't Be Like Alec Baldwin in Glengarry Glen Ross

Remember the famous Glengarry Glen Ross speech delivered by Alec Baldwin? "ABC—Always Be Closing!" The hard sell, all the time.

Not in social media. If it's always about you and your books, it gets tiresome fast. You may think you're doing a numbers game, like sales folk, who cold call with the same script over and over until they land a fish.

In social media, the key word is "social" as in "relating to or designed for activities in which people meet each other for beneficial exchange."

Don't be repetitive, sending the same tweet or message over and over again: *Please follow me on my fan page.* Followed a day later by, *Please follow me on my fan page.* You might as well type *Apply directly to the forehead* because that's what people will want to do with the headache you've given them.

Try to give each message a unique spin or angle. You're a writer, aren't you? Prove it.

3. Use the 80/20 Rule

Spend 80% of your social media time focusing outward. Interact with people. Provide good content. Link to other sites and articles of value. Be personable. Make people glad they have you on their list of people to read.

Use only 20% of the time to "sell" something. And even when you do, don't make it a generic "Buy my stuff" (BMS) kind of thing. If you do BMS over and over again, people are going to tire of you and find ways to avoid your posts.

Instead, always provide some sort of *reason* people should buy your stuff. Maybe it's the launch, which you can announce winsomely and with a little panache. Or a contest. Or you're providing some proof of value (such as a clip of a review). You can be clever in how you word things. Anything but "Buy my stuff!"

4. Don't Hurt Your Writing Time or Your Life

If you find your social media presence detracting from your writing time and your ability to produce quality words, cut back. If you're on Facebook more than you're with your family, check your priorities. This stuff isn't as important as either of those two things.

5. Don't Sweat It

No one knows what works. In fact, even the stuff that works doesn't work all the time. This is a fluid and un-measurable sea we're in. So find a good balance, provide quality, be consistent and be patient.

Most of all write great books. That's the key to repeat business, which is what makes a career.

Interviews

The following interviews were conducted in 2008, appearing originally in the e-magazine of the International Thriller Writers.

Sandra Brown

Sandra Brown's position in the pantheon of best-selling thriller writers is secure. In fact, after so many *New York Times* bestsellers, you can say it's pretty much etched in granite.

But Brown had no idea this was where she'd end up when she was working as a model and doing the weather for WFAA-TV in Dallas. Especially when she was fired.

"It was devastating at the time," Brown says, "but also the

best thing that ever happened to me. I was urged by my husband to start doing what I'd always said I wanted to do, which was to write fiction. I had some stories already in mind, expanded daydreams that had been percolating for a long time. So the creative process wasn't as difficult as adjusting to being self-employed. I hung out my shingle, so to speak, but what is it exactly that a professional writer does?

"Well, in my case, it meant providing something to entertain the kids (two) while I went into the other room to concentrate on my plot. It meant writing a paragraph or two between snack time, laundry, and skinned knees. But if you want to do something badly enough, you find the time to do it. I'm a self-starter, and I loved the new path I'd chosen. It was more difficult to define and explain my new career to other people."

I asked Brown what some of her essentials were when crafting her page-turners.

"Like all fiction, including suspense and thrillers, character is essential. A writer must create a character that the reader cares about. Even if the main character is the villain, like Forsythe's 'Jackal,' the reader must be captivated by his/her predicament and worried about how he/she is going to get out of it.

"Suspense is another essential. That doesn't necessarily mean the 'Boo!' kind of suspense. Every novel should have suspense. It's the element that keeps the reader turning the pages. I try and pose a question, subliminally, to my reader on the first page if possible, and I withhold the answer to that question until the very final pages. New questions arise along the way, and they're gradually answered as the story unfolds. But that main, overriding question, the one that makes a story out of a mere idea, is the last one to be answered."

After a string of romance novels in the '80s, Brown jumped onto the *New York Times* bestseller list with *Mirror Image* (1990). Did she consciously do anything different with that book?

"The initial idea for *Mirror Image* was that someone who was wrapped in head bandages and believed to be someone else, was told a deadly secret. I had skeptics who didn't think a person could pass themselves off as someone else, or that identities could be mistaken and swapped at the scene of a terrible accident. Yet, since 1990 when that book came out, that very thing has happened numerous times. But whether it's entirely plausible or not, it made a good story! And my criteria has always been: Is it within the realm of possibility? Not necessarily *likely*, but within the realm of possibility. When you think about it, that's pretty vast territory! I can't think of a truly riveting book that doesn't flirt with implausibility. If you want truth, read non-fiction."

Brown's work ethic has not flagged over the years.

"I owe my publisher one book a year. It takes me about nine months of writing to fulfill that contract, and that's a good pace for me. (The other three months, not sequentially, I live my life, do promotion, travel, etc.) I do four drafts of each book. The first two take two to three months apiece. The third about a month. The final read-through a couple of weeks.

"I'm not a morning person. I get to the office (outside my house) around 9:30 and stay till around 6:00. I'm not writing all that time. There's a lot of administrative stuff required to run the business, which isn't my favorite thing. I much prefer the writing. Twice a year, I go away, lock myself in, and write for several weeks with as little interruption as possible. I love those times when I can become totally immersed in the story."

I asked Brown about the genesis of *Smash Cut*, which features a villain obsessed with Hitchcockian reenactments.

"It's been a long-standing habit within my family—all of us movie buffs—to drop quotes from favorite films into our conversations. We can quote entire scenes sometimes. I took that game of ours and asked myself what if a film fanatic not only quoted movie scripts, but began acting out scenes? That was the premise that I built the story around.

"Researching *Smash Cut* was great fun. I watched a lot of movies, sometimes replaying a scene again and again so I could get the quote word-for-word correct. Most challenging was finding a murder scene I could use at the story's climax. I polled every movie fan I knew to suggest one. Most of those submitted were grisly scenes—but my villain wasn't about grisly.

"I was conducting my own search for that all-important scene when I came across *Frenzy*. I'd never seen that Hitchcock film, so I ordered it. The one murder scene the audience experiences is so disturbing, I couldn't replicate it! It's discussed in the book, but I just couldn't bring myself to reenact it. I wimped out!"

Brown's novel *Rainwater* was somewhat of a departure for her, but earned excellent reviews.

"I wrote the first draft of *Rainwater* between finishing *Smoke Screen* and beginning *Smash Cut*. Between drafts of *Smash Cut* I'd get it out and work on it when I could afford the time without jeopardizing my delivery of *Smash Cut*. It was worth the extra effort. This is a very different book from my thrillers. It's set in Depression era Texas."

Visit www.sandrabrown.net for more.

Douglas Preston and Lincoln Child

It happened this way.

In 1985 Lincoln Child was an editor at St. Martin's press and a habitué of the American Museum of Natural History. He wanted to do a book on the place and thought an employee named Douglas Preston had the goods to help him.

A lunch at New York's famed Russian Tea room resulted in the two teaming for a non-fiction book, *Dinosaurs in the*

Attic. A friendship was born, and also a longstanding collaboration on a string of bestselling thrillers including *Relic, Still Life With Crows, Mount Dragon* and *Riptide.*

I caught up with the team via three way email.

JSB: What strengths does your partner bring to the table?

DP: Linc has an excellent sense of pacing and plot, far more refined than mine. Having been a systems analyst, as well as a motorcyclist and parrot fancier among other things, he has specialized knowledge of computers, cryptography, motorcycles, parrots, obscure English poetry, and a wide range of other arcane and esoteric subjects. Not to mention his seriously twisted sense of humor . . .

LC: Doug has an almost inexhaustible fund of imagination for drawing up new and imperishable characters. He has a tremendous work ethic and is never satisfied with less than his absolute best. His literary output is remarkably reliable in both extent and quality. He also knows more about more branches of science than anyone I've ever met — and not just dry or technical scientific fact, either, but fascinating anecdotes and conjectures and historical curiosities.

JSB: What lessons have you learned about writing suspense between that first book and the latest?

DP: Many years ago, my friend Stuart Woods gave me an invaluable piece advice: Every chapter, no matter what else it does, has to advance the plot. You have to launch the book like a rocket. You need characters the reader cares about. You have to surprise the reader. And you need to tap into an atavistic human fear. Accomplish these things and you will have a successful story.

LC: I've learned that when it comes to writing a suspense novel, it is important to craft the kind of story you yourself would like to read—rather than what you might assume (cynically or otherwise) is the thriller du jour, or the kind of book that happens to be presently sitting on the bestseller list. Instead of using those as models, I ask myself: What was it that made a certain personal favorite novel stand out in my memory? How was the story developed, and what made it so effective? Since the first tale was told around some prehistoric campfire to keep people from worrying about the man-eaters prowling the darkness beyond, storytelling all comes down to entertainment: and then as now good entertainment takes imagination, skilled pacing, and economy of delivery.

JSB: Doug, tell us a bit about your solo book, *The Monster of Florence*. How were you drawn to this story, and what was the effect of writing it on you?

DP: I moved to Italy with my family as a kind of adventure—and because I had an idea to write a murder mystery set in Florence. I discovered that the olive grove beyond the gates of our villa had been the scene of one of the most horrific double-murders in Italian history. That's how I first learned of the serial killer known as the Monster of Florence, who had never been caught. I eventually gave up the novel and devoted myself to finding out more about the Monster. I teamed up with a

Florentine journalist, Mario Spezi, who had covered the Monster killings from the beginning for the local paper. Mario had a huge archive on the case and knew everyone involved. Together we set out to learn the truth. We eventually tracked down a suspect, interviewed him, and asked him: Are you the Monster of Florence? Lemme tell you, that was some interview . . .

What should have been the end of the story was only the beginning. After that, Mario and I fell into the story, so to speak. I was eventually asked to leave Italy, while Mario was arrested and jailed for murder. It's a story that is so improbable, so bizarre that I'd never dare write it as a novel. But it's all true.

The great thing about being a writer is that you can exorcise a bad experience by writing about it.

JSB: Lincoln, what drew you to your recent solo novel, *Terminal Freeze*?

LC: Ever since I first read Lovecraft's *At the Mountains of Madness* as a boy, I've been entranced by the Arctic/Antarctic setting as a vehicle for a thriller (or, perhaps more aptly, chiller). I've always wanted to write a story set in such a spot. Many of my books seem to focus on a group of people stuck in a distant, dangerous locale in which there is no source of outside help. Certainly the frigid northern wastes of Alaska (in my case, the fictitious Federal Wilderness Zone, or "Zone") provided just such an atmosphere.

I was also intrigued by the challenge of taking a

quintessential "campfire story" and making it my own. Ever since we lived in caves and drew rock paintings instead of surfing the Net, man's most atavistic fear has been of being hunted by something big and fierce and hungry. No secret there—it's a story as old as the hills. But I thought the time had come to see if I could rise to the challenge, write a really unsettling story of that type that could persist in the reader's memory—hopefully—long after the last page has been turned. Genres become classics for a reason, and I felt it was time I did my best to attempt a worthy contribution.

JSB: A lot of new writers would like to know what it takes to get, and stay, published these days. What advice would you give them?

DP: My advice is to understand it's a career, not a book. If the first manuscript doesn't sell, move on to the next. Most successful writers I know (including myself) have an unpublished first novel sitting in a drawer somewhere. You learn how to write a novel by writing a novel.

Staying published is very different from getting published. If you want to stay published—that is, to gain and audience and grow it—give your readers something more than a good story: give them something surprising and different to think about.

LC: These are merely the lessons I've learned myself, rather than some kind of boilerplate advice, because there are no hard and fast rules and no guarantees of success. But here goes: Keep writing. Keep reading, too. Write the kind of books you'd like to read yourself, rather than tailor your work specifically to what you believe to be commercial or salable. You'll have more fun, and readers will tap in to your genuine excitement. Solicit feedback from those whose taste and opinions you trust. Think of each new story or book you write as a learning experience. Feel free to revise it, but chances are you learned so much in the writing process that—if you can't sell it—it's time to try again, building anew on what you've already learned. The publishing industry has contracted, and it's arguably more difficult to get published using the traditional formula, but the rise of the web has given writers an almost unimaginably broad and powerful set of new tools. Leverage those to your advantage. And good luck!

Jonathan Kellerman

Jonathan Kellerman's publishing history shows that he hit the ground running with his first novel, *When the Bough Breaks,* which won several awards and landed on the New York Times bestseller list. But just as in his books, there is a more complex web behind the scenes.

"Actually, *When the Bough Breaks* was my ninth or tenth novel," Kellerman explains. "I wrote a slew of unpublished 'masterpieces' over a thirteen year dry period. The process began in 1971 after I won a writing award in college, got an agent, and began to believe literary success was imminent. Alas, *Bough* wasn't bought until 1983 and publication was delayed to 1985 because the publisher, Atheneum, had no idea what to do with it."

Suffice to say, Kellerman did not have high hopes for his debut.

"The book was purchased as (what I now realize was) a small book destined for a quick death and an unceremonious burial. The advance came out to three bucks an hour and at the time I was making considerably more as a med school professor, clinical psychologist, and court consultant. So I never really thought writing would be a job. It was just something I loved and I figured I'd continue seeing patients and turn out a book every few years, if I could afford the time."

Still, the fact of publication was "proof that I wasn't just a self-deluded neurotic typing away in an unheated garage without a speck of success."

But then the thing all authors hope for happened.

"Somehow — I still don't understand it — the book became a word-of-mouth bestseller. I said, Hmm, okay, let's try another. Same deal. Ditto for my third, fourth, fifth . . . twenty-five years and 30 or so bestsellers later, I still don't get it. But I sure love it and I'm deeply grateful to my readers."

How did Kellerman prepare for this? What foundation was laid down for ultimate bestsellerdom?

"My preparation was being a curious fellow, having a hyperactive imagination and, most important, writing constantly, since the age of nine. It's just something that's always felt right — what psychologists term 'ego-syntonic.'

I was the kid who won the essay contests, penned the school plays, ghost-wrote everyone else's compositions. In college I worked as a cartoonist, reporter, columnist and editor, but my primary goal was to become a clinical psychologist."

Kellerman's creation, Alex Delaware, is now one of the longest running series characters in all crime fiction. I asked Kellerman what he did to keep the character fresh for the readers.

"I don't begin writing a book until I'm excited myself," Kellerman said. "If it doesn't keep me up at night, it won't keep my readers up. Some novels take years to conceive. I'd like to think that my background as a psychologist has helped enrich my stories and I do spend a lot of time devising complex plots and creating suspense. But readers tell me what they like are the characters and characterizing is certainly the most enjoyable element for me."

I also wanted to know what Kellerman's "non-negotiables" are for writing a compelling novel.

"I never really thought in those terms. In fact, I never spend much time trying to figure out what works and what doesn't. Nor do I attempt to write commercially or with an audience in mind. I allow interesting stories and characters to float into my head. Gradually, a plot coalesces, then I do a lot of thinking and researching and outlining until I'm ready to sit down to write the darn thing."

There are, however, some things Kellerman does *not* like in a novel.

"I despise books where murder and violence are taken lightly, because during my psychology days I had many opportunities to witness the effects of violence, and they're anything but cute. And if someone sends me another galley about a psychologically bruised serial-killer hunting a former FBI agent named Kat . . . but apart from that, I really don't have any rules. I suppose any good novel needs to be a mystery in the sense that the reader should want to turn the page to find out what happens next. I do like a strong story catalyzed by serious events, not just minor league angst. I don't have anything against what P. G. Wodehouse termed 'the kind of book where people sit around talking for 200 pages. Then the adolescent doesn't kill himself.' I just don't want to write one."

What Kellerman writes is flat out bestsellers, one after another. How does he do it? Here is a glimpse of a typical Kellerman writing day.

"I get up when I feel like it (a luxury since the kids are grown) which can be anywhere from six-thirty to nine. Shuffle downstairs, mutter bleary greetings to Faye [his wife, bestselling author Faye Kellerman] who is distressingly awake, chipper, gorgeous, and has accomplished more while I snoozed than most people do in a month. Drink coffee, hang out with my beautiful wife for awhile, walk over to the home gym and pretend to be fit, shower, shave, dress, head for the office, turn off the phone, lock the door, rewrite yesterday's work of genius which has now paled considerably in the cold light of morning. Try not to groan. Finally, segue to new stuff. Try to get five good pages down or until my typing falls apart and my head throbs, whichever comes first. Break for lunch, do a bit more writing, then play guitar, do some business, answer fan mail, hang with the granddaughter. If there's any energy left, I like to paint in oils. All the while I'm thinking about my book-in-progress during those zillions of nano-moments when nothing else is occupying my consciousness."

I wondered who Kellerman would choose if he could have any writer from the past sit down and look at his work with a blue pencil.

"No one! Everyone's got their own voice. I'm hard enough on myself without adding to the Delphic chorus of naysayers."

Not many naysayers out there for the work of Jonathan Kellerman, whose latest, *True Detectives,* debuted at #1 on the New York Times list.

So what kept Kellerman going during that thirteen-year dry spell? "A while back I delivered the keynote address at the American Psychological Association's national conference. I faced a couple of thousand shrinks and my first words were, 'I stand before you today as proof of the value of obsessive-compulsive personality.'"

Barry Eisler

[**Note**: This interview was conducted before Eisler made

his famous move, walking away from a $500,000 advance to self-publishing. At the time I called this "The Eisler Sanction."]

We've all heard the admonition "Write what you know." So how can you write about things like covert operations, martial arts and international thrills? Well, research, of course.

Or you can be Barry Eisler.

Trained as a lawyer, then a CIA covert op, Eisler has also been a business exec in Japan and, along the way, earned a black belt in Judo.

So his status as the bestselling writer of the John Rain thrillers seems to have been, well, nearly inevitable. Especially when you consider what attracted him as a kid.

"I have a long-standing interest in what I like to think of as 'forbidden knowledge,'" Eisler explains. "Like methods of unarmed killing, lock picking, breaking and entry, spy stuff, and other things that the government wants only a few select individuals to know. When I was a kid I read a biography of Harry Houdini, and in the book a cop was quoted as saying, 'It's fortunate that Houdini never turned to a life a crime, because if he had he would have been difficult to catch and impossible to hold.' I remember thinking how cool it was that this man knew things that people weren't supposed to know, things that gave him special power. Anyway, since then I've amassed a small and unusual library on some of the foregoing and on other esoteric subjects, I spent three years in the CIA, I got pretty into a variety of martial arts."

When Eisler moved to Tokyo to train in judo, all this material building up in his mind was "like dry tinder, waiting for the spark which life in Tokyo came to provide. Because while I was there commuting to work one morning, a vivid image came to me of two men following another man down Dogenzaka street in Shibuya. I still don't know where the image came from, but I started thinking about it. Who are these men? Why are they following that other guy? Then answers started to come: They're assassins. They're going to kill him. But these answers just led to more questions: Why are they going to kill him? What did he do? Who do they work for? It felt like a story, somehow, so I started writing, and that was the birth of John Rain and *Rain Fall.*

"What's strange, and probably fortuitous, is that I didn't move to Japan with intention or even idea of writing a novel there. I actually just went to train in judo at the Kodokan, to learn Japanese, and to experience first-hand a country and culture that I found fascinating. I think what happened is that living in Tokyo, which for me was a love-at-first-sight experience, catalyzed and expanded on a number of notions that were already lurking in my unconscious."

I asked Eisler about his literary influences.

"I love Trevanian, whose killers Nicolai Hel (in *Shibumi*) and Jonathan Hemlock (in *The Eiger Sanction* and *The Loo Sanction*) are sympathetic in part because they are superior human beings — superior in intellect, taste, and culture.

Andrew Vachss, with his dark, gritty Burke novels and hard-boiled atmosphere, has also been an influence. Pat Conroy and Dave Gutterson have inspired me with the lyricism of their prose. The cadences and imagery of T.S. Eliot and Cormac McCarthy are certainly influences, as well. Stephen King has inspired me with his humor and honesty, and his admonition that the author's job is to tell the truth."

In his thrillers, Eisler favors "realistic action and tradecraft, exotic locations, compelling characters, current political backstory, and steamy sex. There are three general ways to get to know someone's character: time, stress, and sex. In a novel, you don't have time, meaning you need an accelerant, and that leaves you with sex or stress. Violence is one of the most stressful experiences we humans can face, which is why violence can be such a powerful tool in stories. But sex is also enormously revealing, which is why the biblical euphemism that Abraham *knew* Sarah is so apt."

In addition to his writing acumen, Eisler is also known to both established and aspiring writers as a fount of wisdom on the business side of publishing.

"Oh man, this is a huge and vital subject and I could go on about it for pages. Actually, I have gone on about it for pages, and for anyone who's interested in my thoughts on all aspects of marketing and selling, including creating and maintaining a brand; how to get the most out of social networking sites like Facebook; how to choose a winning title (something I've learned the hard way); how to implement an effective and cost-effective tour; how to package a book; the sales cycle; how to recruit your publisher; and why you should see yourself not just as a writer but also as an entrepreneur, you find a lot on the For Writers pages of my website (www.barryeisler.com)."

I like to hear about the typical writing day of successful authors, and asked Eisler about his:

"I wish there were typical days! I just write when I can—promotion is a huge part of the business. I find there's a ratio between thinking and writing, and when I'm just getting started on a book, the ratio is skewed heavily toward thinking, but as the story progresses and I figure things out, I can write more and need to think less. By the time I've reached the last ten percent of the book, I've discovered the whole story out and it's pure writing—an electrifying feeling, like I've grabbed the back of a comet and am struggling just to hang on.

"So at the start of things, I spend a lot time walking and thinking, and a 500 word day feels great. In the middle, I feel comfortable with 1000 or so and I'm spending more time in front of the computer. 2000 always feels good. By the last third of the book, my average gets closer to 3000 and I'm spending close to eight hours a day writing, with sanity breaks mixed in here and there. The most I've ever written in a day (22 straight hours), with my fingers a blur and my hair on fire, was 8200—the last two of which, not coincidentally, were 'The End.'"

Eisler's first standalone thriller, *Fault Line*, is about to hit, and gave him the chance to use more of his background.

"*Fault Line* draws on the same CIA experience I used in writing the Rain books, but also incorporates my subsequent life as a technology attorney and startup executive in Silicon Valley. It was hugely satisfying to use my time in intelligence to craft the character of Ben Treven, a 'Military Liaison Element' (Google this if you want to read a fascinating and underreported story) tasked to 'find, fix, and finish on' Global War on Terror targets. And it was equally pleasing to use my time in law and technology to shape Ben's younger brother, Alex, an ambitious, up-and-coming Silicon Valley technology lawyer and Ben's opposite in experience, temperament, and worldview.

"Much as I've loved writing all the Rain books, it was a special delight to create an entirely new universe of characters in *Fault Line*. Not just Ben and Alex, but also the beautiful, conflicted Iranian-American attorney Sarah Hosseini, whose presence exacerbates the brothers' caustic resentments and who becomes the fulcrum around which all three of them must change if they're to survive the forces they're up against — and to survive each other.

"I'm excited by several traditional genre elements in this story: realistic operator tactics and action (again, drawing on my own CIA experience); exotic locations (the world of Silicon Valley venture capital and high tech law, and Istanbul, which like all the locations I use in my novels I visited for onsite research); sexual antagonism, and fulfillment, between one of the brothers and Sarah.

"But it's the non-genre elements that have me most fired up about this book: the tortured relationship between the brothers; the effect on a culture of a permanent state of war; the events that tear families apart, and the ties that hold them together. *Fault Line* is my most ambitious book yet, and I think my most successful. I had a blast writing it and hope my first standalone will be a hit with Rain fans and with new readers, too."

Joseph Finder

One does not often associate a bestselling thriller writer with the Whiffenpoofs, Yale's storied *a cappella* singing group. But then, one does not come across a background like Joseph Finder's too often.

After a childhood spent with his family in Afghanistan and the Philippines, Finder ended up back in the states. He went on to graduate from Yale *summa cum laude* and Phi Beta Kappa, and got a Masters in Russian studies at Harvard — where he also taught for a time.

Then, at 24, he published his first book, a non-fiction expose of Dr. Armand Hammer and his ties to the Soviet Union. From here he turned to fiction, with *The Moscow Club* (1991). He's been at it ever since. His most recent bestseller is *Power Play* (2007).

The first thing I wanted to know was what Finder does differently as a thriller writer today than when he started.

"The basics of what I do remain the same," Finder says. "I try to tell a gripping story with fast pace, heroes you want to root for, characters who have interesting back stories, and inside information you can't get anywhere else."

But it took Finder a few books to "evolve my own unique voice. We all start out writing under the spell of one or another writer who's captured our imagination, inspired us to write. Some call that imitation. Others talk about the Anxiety of Influence (my old Yale professor, Harold Bloom, even wrote a book about it). And my early novels were very much influenced by the writers I loved, like Robert Ludlum and Frederick Forsyth."

Also early on, Finder admits being "inhibited" by some stern advice given him by an agent, who told Finder "to get rid of all the funny stuff. Humor undermines suspense, he said. Of course, he was wrong. (Ask Harlan Coben, Nelson DeMille, Stephen King, William Goldman . . . the list goes on and on.) So when I wrote *Paranoia*, I decided to disregard all the advice I'd been given, break all the rules, and write a thriller that was often (deliberately) funny, told in the first person voice of a 26-year-old guy who's sort of a scammer—and didn't have any dead bodies. And it turned out that this was the one that broke through to the *New York Times* hardcover bestseller list."

Ignoring that questionable advice about humor allows Finder to write "in a voice that's more naturally mine— more spare, idiosyncratic, with a sort of sociological/cultural observation that lends my stories a certain real-world texture. I'm a lot more interested in writing about real people rather than superheroes, emphasizing family connections and relationships. Now the world of my novels more closely resembles the real world as I see it, and since they feel real to me, they tend to feel real to my readers too—I think. And I've pared down my storytelling in a more cinematic manner—adopting the compression techniques used in good screenplays and TV writing. I think this makes the novels more accessible without sacrificing the emotional and character depth that I (and, I believe my readers) want."

Finder has carved out a unique suspense niche in the world of big business.

"*It's mine, all mine,*" he jokes. "Well, mostly. It sure doesn't feel like something that's been done to death, like the P.I. novel or the legal thriller, which—given how many other similar novels are out there—need some fresh twist to engage our attention. The other thing, even more important, is that the workplace is where we all spend most of our waking hours, increasingly so. Which means in many ways the workplace has become our family, our home. How could it not be interesting—and full of intrigue? Michael Crichton showed, in *Disclosure*, how scary an office can be when people are conspiring against you. I find so many of the great themes in this setting, including ambition and success, friendship and love—and greed and deceit and betrayal. It's all there."

Another mark of Finder's work is the use of First Person narration. He finds it "more intimate than third-person, more immediately involving. If a writer does it right, he grabs the reader at once. The reader's along for the ride."

But there are challenges. "Unless you're willing to violate the first-person constraints and interject third-person (as I've done), you're limited in how much you can show of the external threat, of what the villain may be plotting or what trouble your hero is about to get into. Also, a first-person narrator is a character in him/herself, so it's all about doing the voice right, because the voice supplies the characterization, so it's got to be consistent and interesting."

Finder keeps a disciplined writing routine which he terms "boring," but is, from the results, highly effective.

"I keep an office outside my home, where I do my research and writing, and where my invaluable assistant comes in four days a week to help out in a thousand ways. I get to work after seeing my daughter off to school (or driving the carpool when it's my turn), and then I write for several hours, take a break, check my email (an evil, evil thing email has become: the great Time Suck), write some more, go work out, grab lunch, and then do business in the afternoon. Sometimes I make calls for research then, but more often I spend the afternoon on non-writing business. When a book is really rocketing along, though, I often extend my writing day by getting up insanely early — 4:00 in the morning, say — and logging in a few hours on my home computer before going to the office.

"The big news for me — which will show you how dull my life is, if this is the big news — is that I've just finished the first of a planned series, with one continuing hero. My publisher has been asking me for years to write a series character, and so have a lot of my readers, but I kept resisting. I had no interest in doing a police homicide detective, not while Michael Connelly is doing Harry Bosch. Nor an FBI agent or a CIA officer. I wanted to keep writing stories set in the world of *Paranoia* and *Killer Instinct* and *Power Play*, and I didn't know how I could bring a continuing character into such a setting. Then one day I met someone who does super-secret international investigations for corporations and politicians and governments, extremely discreet and extremely interesting, and I realized I'd found my character. I named my hero Nick Heller, and I'm already on book two of his adventures, and I'm enjoying it immensely."

Peter Straub

Peter Straub has achieved that enviable position of both critical and commercial success. Perhaps that's because, when he started, he faced the dilemma of needing to earn a living while desiring to take his writing beyond genre conventions.

"Essentially, I try to write as if there is no distinction between literary and commercial fiction," Straub says. "When I began, finding readers was very important to me. I wanted to be able to support myself with my writing, which meant that I had to sell a good number of books. At the same time, I wanted to write as well as I could, to do interesting things with structure and point of view, to create characters who were real human beings in real-world contexts. I wanted the reader to smell the cut grass, to see the undersides of leaves, to feel the earth underfoot."

The author of such acclaimed novels as *Ghost Story, Shadowlands* and *Koko*, Straub has never lost a certain sense of play in his writing.

"One of my central concerns has been to ground the elements of horror and suspense in a firmly novelistic context. After that, I just tried to have a kind of fun, a kind of pleasure, in using the devices of metafiction, intertexuality, conflicting realities, shattered points of view, false endings, unreliable narrators, tonal shifts, whatever I could think of. My assumption going in was that horror was capable of doing anything and everything, that there were no real limitations or boundaries to it."

Straub has also collaborated with Stephen King on two projects, *The Talisman* and *Black House*. Not a bad writing partner. So I asked Straub, if he could collaborate with any other writer in history, besides King, who would he choose?

"I am happy to say that I cannot imagine collaborating with any other writer than Stephen King, who simply cannot be bettered at the task of maintaining support, joyfulness, cooperation, and inspiration during the long and difficult business of writing a novel. With anyone else, I think the results would be disastrous as fiction and fatal to whatever level of friendship I had with the other party. I mean, who would I pick? Raymond Chandler? Jack Kerouac? I love them, but could we work together? Hmm, the Magic 8-Ball is saying, 'Not on your life, bud.' Oh, I know, actually. I pick Shakespeare. He could write us out any hole I put us in, and I could learn a tremendous amount. At the end of the day, we could go to the pub together. I don't want to ask him any questions, I just want to hear him talk."

Straub's upcoming release is *A Dark Matter*. It has its roots in the crazy '60s, which Straub felt compelled to draw upon.

"The people I remembered were the wandering philosopher-freeloaders who began to appear on college campuses and in places like Haight-Ashbury in the mid-sixties. They attracted circles of admirers, followers, stooges, who supported them and listened to their endless explanations of everything under the sun. These guys were usually aged from 30 to 35, still young, but enough older than their victims to possess a kind of authority. They had sex with the good-looking girls, they were fed, they clothed themselves with the shirts and trousers of their male admirers. They lifted your jazz records and gave them to someone else. They talked and talked about The Tibetan Book of the Dead, Marcuse, Norman O. Brown, conspiracies, Buddhism, the apocalypse, drugs, politics. The 60s were filled with these phonies, rancid with them. Any account of the 60s that does not include them is incomplete.

"So I thought I'd write about the chaos left in the wake of one of these characters."

Straub continues a steady literary pace. I asked him about his "typical" writing day.

"These days, I am no longer capable of the ten-hour stretches I used to put in, day after day, night after night. My work day begins around 11 in the morning and there is a break for lunch around 1:30 or 1:45. At 2:00, while eating lunch, I wander through Llanview, PA, an amazing little city where anything can happen: amnesia, resurrections, dopplegangers, serial killers, arson, rapes, visitations from the heavenly realms . . . I'm telling you, in Llanview they live life with a capital L. At 3:30 or thereabouts, I return to my desk and work till about 7:00. If I get in five hours of work, it's a good day, and I know I've had it until the next time."

Stephen Coonts

Can you say "overachiever"?

Stephen Coonts, author of 15 *New York Times* bestsellers, grew up in a coal-mining town of 6,000 on the western slope of the Appalachian Mountains. After graduating from West Virginia University in 1968, he was commissioned as an Ensign in the U.S. Navy.

He received his Navy wings in 1969 and made two combat cruises aboard the USS Enterprise during the final years of the Vietnam War. He left active duty in 1977 and got a degree from University of Colorado School of Law in 1979.

After a few years of law practice he wrote his first novel, *Flight of the Intruder,* which was published by the Naval Institute Press in 1986. It spent twenty-eight weeks on the *New York Times* bestseller list, and was made into a movie released in 1991.

Pause for breath.

That first novel enabled Coonts to turn to writing full time. Which he does now, in Colorado, when he isn't flying planes with his wife, Deborah.

"The success of *Flight of the Intruder* was unexpected and certainly caught me by surprise," Coonts says. "I was practicing law for an oil company at the time and it was in financial trouble. I decided to try to make a living writing, and fortunately it worked out. The publishers wanted another Jake Grafton tale, then another, and I was off and running. I tell people I haven't done a lick of honest work from that day to this. It's been one big lie after another."

Coonts has also written three other series, which "keeps me fresh."

"Jake Grafton put my kids through college, paid for the planes and flying, and paid for the farm. But *Saucer* and its sequel have kept me enjoying the writing process. The *Deep Black* series is pure action-adventure, pulp fiction as an art form, and it's fun too. I wrote *The Cannibal Queen*, a nonfiction flying adventure, for the same reason. And there is a contemporary novel, *The Garden of Eden*, that my publisher reluctantly published, but only under a penname. The challenge of doing different things is that your audience usually refuses to try something different. People buy the brand and are loyal to it, and it's hell getting them to try another flavor. Finally, there is the reality of modern publishing: Computers neither forget nor forgive. You are only as good as the sales of your last book, whatever it was. You step outside your brand at your peril."

This prodigious output gives Coonts a singular perspective in the challenge of series characters.

"I think if you use the same characters over and over, they have to grow as human beings or the series will slowly lose its audience," he says. "Series burnout, the publishers call it. Finding new plots that can be written with on-going characters can be very difficult."

That being said, what does Coonts do to keep up the quality of his writing?

"Doing other things now and then to keep the enthusiasm level high. It helps that my wife loves action-adventure and is a gushing fountain of plot ideas. She has become a huge resource for me as a writer."

As for the writing life itself, Coonts does not have a set routine. "I don't know that I have ever been fortunate enough to have a typical writing day. If I ever do, it would go something like this: Get up, have coffee with my wife, answer emails, go to breakfast at one of our favorite places or eat it at home, then write until I run dry. Dinner with friends."

Not a bad way to spend a writing life, the latest result of which is *The Assassin,* which debuted at #12 on the *New York Times* list.

Katherine Neville

It's a bit of a cliché to say that Katherine Neville burst on the scene with her first published novel, *The Eight* (1988). But in her case it's absolutely true. To an extent. "In reality it was fifteen years from spark to ARC," Neville says.

The spark happened during an actual "dark and stormy night" in the 1970s, when Neville was working in Algeria. "I'd been exiled there by my employer, an international consulting firm, and I had just learned that one of our clients, OPEC, had decided to declare an international embargo on the chief export they controlled: petroleum. I saw this 'Third World' move as something completely new in a global game that had been going on since the end of World War II—a shift in the balance of powers."

At the same time, Algeria was celebrating the tenth anniversary of its successful revolution against France. "The entire scenario reminded me of the French Revolution when all bets were off after the destruction of the nobility, the bourgeoisie, even the proletariat. The picture around me suddenly seemed like a game of chess where an unexpected move had upset the game as well as the rules."

Publishers Weekly called *The Eight* "daring, original and moving" and "destined to become a cult classic." The book was a huge success and now Neville's sequel, *The Fire,* is about to hit the shelves. Early reviews have been raves.

I asked Neville what she had learned about writing thrillers between these two books.

"When it comes to craft, the most important thing I learned through the writing-publishing process was something that isn't taught in any creative writing program, literature department, drama or screenwriting school. It's considered inessential to literary writing. But it's definitely essential to writing thrillers, adventure stories, horror, mystery, crime—you name it. In a word, *Pacing*."

Neville says she learned about pacing only after writing her books and working directly with some of the best editors in the business.

"The first major editor I worked with, when I asked him what pacing was, told me, 'I don't know how to define it or explain it for you. I just know—whatever it is—it's what makes me want to turn the page.' Amen."

Neville's idea-generating process is intuitive, springing directly from the life she leads. "I often say: Life is Research. I go and live in places or do jobs my characters do, to learn about them. The rest is more of an organic process, and that process for me has to begin with a character or characters that I'm interested in enough that I want to spend at least a few years of my life—or 500 pages—living with them. Many of us don't even want to spend that much time with our own friends, colleagues, families, or loved ones!"

In the case of *The Fire*, Neville began with two of the major characters. "I knew well in advance that the character of Xie (daughter of Cat and Solarin from *The Eight*) was highly conflicted about her relationship with each of her parents because she had a special gift or talent that not everyone could understand or relate to enough to help her be able to exercise that gift. The same is true of Charlot, the historic hero (son of Mireille and Talleyrand from *The Eight*). Both of them have gifts that estrange or even frighten people — leaving the two characters as 'outsiders' even to their own families. Never having been a prodigy at anything myself, that was the hardest research I had to do for *The Fire*."

When it comes to plotting, though, Neville does "try to plan everything up front. I know the entire plot and all the characters intimately — and in a perfect world I would even know the last sentence — before I write the first line of a book."

But it is all subject to change. "I admit that when Napoleon or Lord Byron or a child chess prodigy or the Chief of Staff of the US Treasury accidentally drops into my plot or my research, I *always* go wherever the flow suggests."

For new writers, Neville offers the following advice:

1. **Write.** Remember, people may keep you (or me) from being a published author but no one can stop you from being a writer. All you have to do is write. And keep writing. While you're working at a career, while you're raising children, while you're trout fishing — keep writing! No one can stop you but you.

2. **Write *three* books, not *one*.** No publisher wants to gear up the huge machine to promote a one-shot wonder who will never publish another book, no matter how brilliant it may be. Before you get an agent, have at least one novel

completed and more in draft. Stephen King and Steve Berry both demonstrated their prolific natures before becoming commercially successful authors, and that has helped each of them remain successful.

3. **Most important: Write what you love to read!** Otherwise, no one may never get to read it.

Andrew Gross

Unpublished writers are naturally looking for that first break. Even a little crack in the door can be the start of something big.

Rarely, however, are the doors swung open to the throne room from the get-go. But in the case of Andrew Gross, that's exactly what happened.

He was struggling away, producing manuscripts, when an editor saw something in his writing and recommended Gross to none other than James Patterson. Patterson was looking for a co-writer at the time, and called Gross up.

That pairing went on to produce six #1 bestsellers.

Nothing like starting at the top.

So what was it that the editor saw in Andrew Gross? It was his strong women characters. I asked Gross how he developed that talent.

"Could it be fifteen years in the women's apparel business?" he joked. "I don't know. Everybody has their own skills. A strong female who rises to provide the heroic aspect of the book has always been very sexy to me. So I respond to it and it comes naturally. I am also the cook and the 'shopper' in our family, and I'm forced to get pedicures (on pain of not being let into bed!), so I guess I have this tiny, elevated feminine side."

During his collaboration with Patterson, Gross learned how to craft long, detailed outlines. The discipline served him well, though now he's able to shorten the process.

"I do always start with a detailed proposal, which I present to my editor and publisher. It's usually a synopsis of the overriding concept, the main characters, the conflict, where I see it going. At least half the book. I probably also include an outline of the first ten scenes or so, pretty fleshed out. It's important to me they buy in. From that point on, I find myself outlining in segments of ten to fifteen chapters, just to stay ahead of myself. Keep me on task. I know where I want to go, but sometimes don't do the heavy lifting and take the shortcut now that I have several books under me and know the process."

So what is central to an Andrew Gross plot? "It has to have a compelling personal conflict or wound at the heart of the main character—which provides the emotional fuel of the story—and a local, seemingly unrelated event that widens into what's really at stake."

Gross typically starts with "something that has attracted me emotionally, a family torn apart, secrets buried, etc.

Then I try to wrap that around a crime, maybe picked up on the news. I start with the family crisis, and that creates my characters. In my last few books I've been dealing with crimes like hit-and-run and home invasion murders, that widen into national cover-ups and conspiracies. So the big picture payoffs can be taken from the news. But it's the family aspect that provides courage and redemption, the emotional fuel that is universal."

Gross has a typical writing day. He's a "morning guy" who is at his desk by eight. "I do the Face-book, email thing. A little solitaire maybe, then I loop back to yesterday's pages. Because my books tend to be roughly one hundred 3-5 page chapters, I try to crank out a chapter a day. I only come down from my office after I force it out, one chapter, whether it's lunchtime or five p.m."

And what's next for Andrew Gross?

"I just turned in a new thriller set in Greenwich around a conspiracy behind the financial meltdown. I'm going to take a break from Ty Hauck [featured most recently in Don't Look Twice] and do something a bit more personal, a story built around a teenage suicide, which some may know was something we went through with a nephew this year. And back to a first person narrator. Haven't done that since working with Patterson."

Visit Andrew Gross at www.andrewgrossbooks.com.

Lisa Jackson

Lisa Jackson did not start out to kill people. The popular suspense author wanted to write romance.

Though she's always been a mystery/suspense reader, she didn't consider the genre herself when she started out about twenty-seven years ago.

Her sister, writer Nancy Bush, had come to her with the idea of writing romance novels. "Nancy had read an article about young mothers making a livelihood out of doing just that," Jackson recalls. "I thought she was crazy. We both read mystery. To that date, neither of us had read a romance novel, but the next day, as I was babysitting a bunch of little kids, I thought 'Why not?'"

By the time Nancy came to pick up her daughter, Lisa had written the prologue of a novel. That first novel didn't sell, but came back with editorial comments that suggested there was "too much" suspense.

Despite that, when she started selling, she kept putting in suspense, disregarding the "tip sheets" from the publishers.

"Later, as my stories grew longer, I was encouraged to increase the suspense and I couldn't be happier. Now, finally, I'm writing what I love to read, and my sister, also an accomplished author, are finally writing a book together that will be out next year, and guess what? The publisher wants as much suspense as we can stuff into it.

It's true what they say: What goes around, comes around."

I asked Jackson what lessons she brought from the romance genre to her suspense.

"I love a love story within the novel," she says. "And I believe that the love story and emotional commitment of the characters heightens the suspense. The more you love, the more you're vulnerable. Your lover can be used as a pawn against you. I guess the most glaring similarity is the emotional hook to the reader."

And Jackson has certainly hooked a loyal following, with bestsellers that include *Hot Blooded, Cold Blooded* and *Final Scream.*

She's also written in the historical genre, which brings up the question of specialization, or "branding." Must writers stick to a brand these days?

"Hmm . . . that's a good question. On a purely intellectual level, I think a writer should write what he or she wants to regardless of genre. Of course, that doesn't necessarily mean all the books he/she writes will be published. But it keeps the author fresh and, despite branding, not getting into a rut. In my case, most of my historical novels had a suspense/thriller element to them, even serial killers. They were fun. I'm glad I did them. I think a writer should hone his/her skills no matter what the genre."

Jackson describes herself as a "seat-of-the-pants" writer when she's drafting, but works from a detailed synopsis.

"The synopsis is usually 50-60 pages," she says. "I write in spurts and under deadline, not a 10 page a day thing, but I always have a synopsis and I rewrite as I go along—to get the wording write, to add a red herring, to add motivation.

"Writing the synopsis is creating an intense plan that makes my head hurt when I do it. Literally hurt. The synopsis includes enough back story of the characters so that I, and my editor, understand them. It also is a detailed plot that includes red herrings and the twists and turns, even scenes and sometimes dialogue that will show up in the book."

Does she ever deviate from the synopsis?

"Of course. Sometimes I even begin the book in a different place within the plot if I need something more dramatic, but I follow the bones of it. In *Lost Souls*, I started the book in a place I hadn't planned. Once I go forward, though, I try to adhere to the plot as much as possible. This is the skeleton of the book and if I deviate too far, I end up in big trouble. Since I sell my books on the synopses, I need to give the publisher something my editor expects when I deliver the manuscript. Once I start writing the book, however, I do submerge into the plot and I'm really 'there.'"

And when she's "there," she does not have a typical writing day. "When I'm under deadline it's nearly 24-7— well, maybe 18-7, and when I'm not I actually go to the dentist, doctor, have the car washed and go bowling. I always try to get in a little exercise and fun things with friends, but not when a deadline looms. If there's anything that's constant it's that I'm a morning person and write in the mornings."

Visit Lisa's website at www.lisajackson.com

Kathy Reichs

Kathy Reichs works full time for the Office of the Chief Medical Examiner in North Carolina and for the Laboratoire de Sciences Judiciaires et de Medecine Legale for the province of Quebec. She is a Professor in the Department of Sociology and Anthropology at the University of North Carolina-Charlotte, teaches FBI agents at Quantico how to detect and recover human remains, is one of only fifty forensic anthropologists certified by the American Board of Forensic Anthropology, and is on the Board of Directors of the American Academy of Forensic Sciences.

Oh yes, and she also writes bestselling thrillers featuring forensic anthropologist Temperance "Bones" Brennan.

The popularity of "Bones" is well established, evidenced by the Fox TV series of the same name (it debuted in 2005). So I asked Kathy how much backstory she gave Temperance when she wrote her first novel.

"Not very much," Reichs said. "I introduced Tempe as a current character, describing her personality traits, as well as her job as a forensic anthropologist, her role at the lab, her reasons for being in Montreal. I did give her the crumbling marriage and rebellious daughter as recent backstory, and did allude, cryptically, to a colorful part of her past involving an overly close relationship with alcohol."

From another angle, the series character presents a challenge. How do you keep her fresh from book to book? Reichs did not hesitate. "Avoid doing serial killer after serial killer!"

Then, more sedately, she added, "Seriously, each story looks at violence from a different perspective: due to individual psychopathology *(Deja Dead)*, due to collective sociopathology (Death du Jour), for profit (Deadly Decisions). And each has a different message: the misery caused by genocide (Grave Secrets), the cruelty of trafficking in endangered species (Bare Bones), the danger of fanatic religious beliefs (Cross Bones). Also, the characters, and their relationships, must keep evolving, or the reader must continue to learn more and more about them. And the settings, seasons, and crime details change, of course."

Reichs has enjoyed progressive growth as a writer, and an ever-expanding readership. So what has she learned about the craft over the course of her writing career?

"For the first books I did full chapter by chapter outlines," Reichs said. "I don't do that anymore, but use a more free-flow approach. Also, I believe my writing style has become more polished, more economical, with less use (abuse?) of similes and metaphors. I still do all of my own research and writing, though I am fortunate to have the expertise of my colleagues to help me with questions outside the realm of forensic anthropology."

After a moment, Reichs added, "Let me rephrase it. I do keep an outline. But now I tend to do it, still chapter by chapter, as I *finish* each chapter. I still plot the story, but in a less structured way. I start with an outline of the first six chapters or so, and a general overall description of the book's theme and where the story line will go, then I launch in."

That makes her process "circular, not linear. Sometimes a later development forces me to go back and modify earlier sections."

With her full schedule, Kathy Reichs does not have a "typical" writing day. "Since I do not have the luxury of being a full time writer, any day that I am not at the lab, in court, on set in LA, traveling, etc. I write all day. I try to get at the computer by 8 am, stay with it, except for a lunch break, until 5 or 6 pm. During vacation (during what?) I may even write in the morning."

Her fans don't care when she writes, as long as she keeps on doing it.

M.J. Rose

M. J. Rose faced the marketing dragon and decided to slay it on her own.

When her first novel, *Lip Service,* was turned down by several houses because they didn't know how to "position" it, Rose self-published. Because she had a story that needed telling.

"All of my books start with a theme that matters to me, even if my readers don't ever focus on the theme," Rose says. "Why women close their eyes to reality and allow themselves to be swept through life instead of walking through it on their own is both a symptom of our society and a description of Julia Sterling at the beginning of the novel."

Rose spent two years writing *Lip Service,* while working in advertising. "I was scared the whole time that I would fail at creating the characters I could see move and think and speak in my mind, and would fail at pacing the book so that it moved and didn't get bogged down in ideas. Most of all, I was afraid I would fail in telling the truth about this woman and what she goes through."

But the result pleased both Rose and her early readers. "I have been told many times in the ten years since it was published that the book is brave and unflinching, and that is something I'm most proud of."

Rose was on her way as a novelist. *The Memorist,* her tenth novel, has just released. But that doesn't mean the writing comes any easier. "It seems every time I start a book I'm starting all over again, learning all over again. And I'm still scared. About all of the same things except here it's the reincarnation aspects of the book not sexuality that makes me nervous."

The Memorist takes place in the present and two past eras. As a child, Meer Logan was haunted by memories of another time and place always accompanied by the faint strains of elusive music. Her past has reached out again in the form of a strange letter that sets her on a search to unlock the mystery of who she once was. With the help of her father—a Kabbalist, known as the Jewish Indiana Jones—Meer attempts to learn the meaning behind her hauntingly vivid memories. What they discover could reveal a frighteningly powerful secret hidden for generations by one of the greatest composers of all time.

"With each step she comes closer to remembering the connections between a clandestine reincarnationist society," says Rose. "A lost flute linked to Ludwig van Beethoven and David Yalom, a journalist who understands all too well how the past affects the future and who plans to force the word to understand—thorough a single violent act—that those who cannot remember the past are condemned to repeat it."

Rose comes up with her twisting plots this way. "I write five or six days a week. I make a huge effort to not work all seven days—which is all too easy for me to do. I spend one hour thinking about the book in the morning—walking or swimming—planning what I am going to write that day. Where the book is going. Then I write from four to five hours during the first draft process. 12 PM-2PM and then 3PM-6PM. Give or take. In between I take a walk, go get coffee, or talk on the phone. After the first draft (and I usually have three to four drafts) I usually work more than that—from 6-9 hours."

But fiction is not the only thing Rose is known for. Among writers, she's considered an expert in the often frustrating art of marketing a book. On that score, her advice is simple.

"Get the best agent you can, learn as much as you can about the industry, the process and the ways you can be your publisher's partner, invest in your own book and be proactive but remember that you can't go the distance without a publisher backing you—so don't drive yourself crazy over anything but the writing."

James Scott Bell/K. Bennett
Interviewed by Hallie Ephron

"The whole zombie thing is hot now, but it's all the same, zombies as slobbering, mindless monsters. What if the zombie was the hero? In fact, what if it was a lawyer practicing law in L.A.?"

HALLIE EPHRON: That's the question author James Scott Bell (suspense writer, extraordinary writing teacher, and author of the classic, *Plot & Structure*) posed to his agent, the legendary Donald Maass.

Bell spun the idea out further:

"I mean, how can you tell the difference between zombies and defense attorneys anyway? Most people think there IS no difference. And what if this lawyer specialized in defending outcasts like vampires, who never get a break?"

I'm laughing. You're laughing. Donald Maass was laughing. Immediately he wanted a proposal that he could take to publishers and sell.

So Bell put together a pitch and a tagline for the as-yet unwritten novel that would become *Pay Me in Flesh*, the first in the Mallory Caine, Zombie-at-Law series by the "mysterious yet roguishly handsome" **K. Bennett** and published by Kensington.

Tell us the pitch you up with, Jim?

JAMES SCOTT BELL: Here it is--

Tagline: In L.A., practicing law can be hell. Especially if you're dead.

Pitch: In an increasingly hellacious L.A., zombie lawyer Mallory Caine defends a vampire hooker accused of the crime Mallory herself committed, even as a zombie-killer closes in and the love of her former life comes back as the Deputy DA she must oppose. And as Lucifer himself begins setting up L.A. as his headquarters for a new attack on heaven and earth, Mallory slowly discovers she may be the one who has to stop him.

HALLIE: I love it! Truth: How do you craft an amazing pitch like that, and did you have to revise it after you wrote the book?

JAMES SCOTT BELL: Actually, this pitch hasn't changed

since I wrote it. It's exactly what went into the proposal. This is always how I start my novel preparation. I have to have a tagline and a short pitch that is exciting enough for me to believe in the book. If I just start writing I might find out that the foundation is weak. But if I have a strong premise in this form, and I'm jazzed, then I have about half my work done.

I actually enjoy this process. I like thinking like a marketing executive. What sort of thing would go on a movie poster? That's my tagline. And then I want to write back cover copy. What pitch would compel a browser to buy the book?

HALLIE: Tell us about zombies, and what makes one a good lawyer?

JAMES SCOTT BELL: For a zombie to be a good lawyer, she would have to have to have a good law school education and experience in the courtroom. Mallory Caine has both. Unfortunately, she was murdered and brought back to life by someone who wants to control her, and is now one of the walking dead. But not the slobbering kind. Not the cliché monster we see in countless movies and books and TV shows. She's still got a will and she's still got her mind and she will not allow anyone to control her. Yes, she's got to eat human flesh and brains, but no one's perfect. Especially an L.A. lawyer.

HALLIE: I've heard you say that it's not a good idea to "write to the market"—You end up with a book without any soul (not good, even for a zombie novel). So I'm guessing you came up with a plot that you connected with emotionally. Can you tell us how?

JAMES SCOTT BELL: That's exactly right. I've never believed in writing for the market alone. But your agent and the people who are going to pay you for your books do have an eye on the market. The key is to bring a fresh voice to that perspective. That's what you always hear agents and editors say on a panel. They want something unique and fresh with a "voice," but they also want to know that it's something that can sell. You have to put those two dynamics together.

For *Pay Me in Flesh*, the concept jumped out at me. I'd been thinking, What hasn't been done in zombie fiction? So much of it is the same. Then I thought, How about an actual legal thriller where the lawyer just happens to be a zombie? All sorts of intriguing possibilities started to pop up.

And then I went into my character work. I knew I wanted the lawyer to be a woman helping low level paranormals with their problems. One of the first things I do with a major character is a Voice Journal. I start a free-form document, stream of consciousness, in the voice of the character. I let the voice begin to develop on its own. When it starts to speak to me in a unique way, with attitude and singularity, I know I'm on the right track. That's when I start to connect with the character.

Then I need to bond with the character emotionally. I build some backstory for that. When I find myself thinking about the character when I'm not writing, I know I'm close to getting started.

HALLIE: Why the pseudonym?

JAMES SCOTT BELL: Simply for brand differentiation. I've got a strong readership under my own name, and this is a launch into a whole new genre. I'm not making it a secret. I just want readers to know from the cover what kind of book it is.

HALLIE: Love how you describe your doppelgänger and nom de plume: "K. Bennett boxed Golden Gloves and worked as a bouncer in Hell's Kitchen before turning to fiction, and often imagines the past in terms that are not entirely truthful." Really?

JAMES SCOTT BELL: The cool thing about a pen name is I get to make up a whole new personality. At one time I did want to be a boxer, so I gave that bit of backstory to K. Bennett—and then dropped in the "less than truthful" part. I never boxed Golden Gloves or bounced in Hell's Kitchen, except in my dreams. But now I get to put my dreams into a bio.

[Originally appeared on the website www.junglered.com]

Self-Publishing

Well, even as I write this, and even as I prepare to put out this e-book, and even as I upload the thing—everything is in flux. Who knows what the landscape will look like even a month from now? Or a year?

One thing is certain, though. This is what I call a "golden age" for writers. Some time ago I put that opinion into a blog comment box, and received a rejoinder to the effect that there was so much junk being put out there, times really aren't "golden" for most. It was a good challenge, so I took it up, and reproduce here what I wrote:

In the "old days" (i.e., before November 2007!) it was not only extremely difficult to get published, it was a virtual certainty that even getting published would not make you a living (I'm speaking specifically about fiction writers). I think there was some stat along the lines of five grand a year being the AVERAGE a published fiction writer made.

A few were able to break into the top tier, but not many. The midlist was the largest population of professional fictioneers.

But a lot of talented writers never got into the walls of the Forbidden City, or, if they did, weren't able to hold a place there (or were consigned to wandering minstrel duty). The money counters made the decisions inside the walls, not the writer.

It could take years for a writer holding a full time day job to work on his project and maybe get a chance at going to market. Still, the overwhelming majority of such projects never found a home. The Forbidden City can hold only so many within its ramparts.

But now, what ho, out in the dark forest there are campfires all over the place, and people finding storytellers there. All sorts of them. And they are more than willing to shell out ducats to the ones they like. The really good tale spinners do not have to wait years for a chance at the City. They can get paid right now, and some may even make what begins to resemble a living. And note: That number is larger than was ever possible before under the old system.

More writers than ever are making real gold from their writing. Thus: a golden age!

Now, it is quite true that there are those who will not be filling their money purses even though they've got several fires going. Some of these are not true "writers," but those seeking quick bucks or just think anyone can do this. Such may seem to overrun the forest. But they will soon leave, discouraged or dissuaded.

But for real writers, those who care about their craft, what is not to like about this? As I point out in my book on self-publishing, a steady income stream can be created if one melds talent, craft and a modicum of systemization into a continuous output. It's happening every month, for more and more scribes. And here's the bonus: the gates to the Forbidden City may open yet! An invitation may still be issued (i.e., self-publishing no longer carries a stigma).

Now the storyteller has a choice. Take a deal from the Forbidden City, or continue as he is doing, telling stories for ducats, making up new ones as he sees fit and offering them up right away. Perhaps it will be a blend of the two systems, a real creative partnering. But the point is it's now a true choice, a real choice, something that was not open for writers under the old system.

There is gold AND opportunity, in other words, for writers, unlike anything we've ever seen since old Gutenberg monkeyed with his winepress. Yes indeed: a golden age!

Now I have to go work on my novel.

[And so, what follows are some of the comments and posts I've made about self-publishing. For a system that increases the chances of making steady income over time, please see my book *Self-Publishing Attack!*]

Declaration of Indie-Pendence

When in the course of business events, it becomes necessary for writers to dissolve the exclusive bands which have connected them to an industry, and to assume among the powers of the earth, the separate and equal station to which the laws of creativity and of creativity's Source entitle them, a decent respect for the opinions of reading kind requires that they should declare the causes which compel them to a new way of doing business.

We hold these truths to be self-evident, that all writers are created to tell stories, that they are endowed by their imaginations with certain unalienable rights, that among these are writing books, getting them published and making some dough. That to secure these rights, distribution systems are instituted, deriving their just powers from the consent of the marketplace. And that whenever an alternative system arises that provides writers with potential additional income, it is the right of those writers to choose to see what gives.

Prudence, indeed, will dictate what the best path is to pursue. But that there are different paths now is a fact, and the writer is free to further his career and earn a living in whatever way seems fittest and most just.

Let certain facts be submitted to a candid world:

– There is now no one way to publish, and there never will be again.

– The traditional publishing industry is still viable, but must become more flexible toward writers.

– Writers and their agents must assume a greater and more informed vigor in negotiations. Editors and industry reps must be equally prepared to negotiate, for it is in their long term interest to nurture new writers. Without new writers, there will be no traditional industry left.

– The new term for traditional publishing should be "creative partnership." And both those words should be taken seriously.

– Writers who are traditionally published must begin to set aside the gentle fantasy that they are better than self-published writers *by definition.*

– Self-published writers must set aside their unbridled lust to set fire to the walls of the Forbidden City and bay at the moon.

– Writers of any stripe must continue to hone their craft and write the best books they can. Every time out. No exceptions.

We writers, therefore, appealing to the supreme value of independence and creativity, do solemnly declare that we are free; that we are absolved from all allegiance to one way of doing things, and that as full, free and responsible beings we have the right to enter into any deal we think is best. That may be indie publishing. That may be traditional publishing. It may be a mix of both. But it will be a free choice.

For the support of this declaration, with firm reliance on the power of the written word, we mutually pledge to each other—and the reading public—our books, our stories and our sacred calling.

5 *Things Every Writer Needs to Understand About Self-Publishing*

So now you are either self-publishing or thinking about self-publishing.

Yes, welcome to the world of everybody.

I have a question for you. Do you actually want to make some money at it?

Here's the good news: Your ficus can make money self-publishing. Your cat, Jingles, can make money self-publishing.

Of course, by *money* we are talking about enough scratch to buy some Bazooka at your local 7-Eleven. Or maybe a Venti White Chocolate Mocha at Starbucks. That's not bad. It's *something*.

But if you want to make some real dime, and keep it coming, there are a few things you need to understand.

1. You are going into business

The authors who are making significant money self-publishing operate with sound business principles. Which makes many other authors as nervous as Don Knotts.

"I'm just not wired that way!" they'll say. "I want to concentrate on my writing! I haven't got the time or inclination to think about business decisions."

But guess what? Even if you have a traditional publishing contract, you're going to have to give time and attention to business, namely marketing.

What if you spent a little of that same time and effort learning the principles of successful self-publishing?

Of course, a lot of authors now want to go right into digital. Well, don't do it until you fully understand that it's a business you're going to be running. That business is you.

Learn how. The basics are not that hard.

2. Your mileage will vary

No one can replicate another author's record. Each author and body of work is unique. Innumerable factors play into the results, many of which are totally out of the control of the writer.

If you go into self-publishing expecting to do as well as author X, you'll be setting yourself up for disappointment.

Instead, concentrate on being the best provider of content *you* can be. See #5, below.

3. This isn't get rich quick

In the "early days" of the e-book era, those who jumped in with both feet (Amanda Hocking, Joe Konrath, John Locke) and those who had loads of backlist (Bob Mayer) or caffeinated series ideas (Lee Goldberg) got some nice returns.

Now, the future for the overwhelming majority of writers is about quality production, consistently and over time. A long time. Which is fine if you love to write.

4. You can't just repeat "buy my stuff" and expect to sell any of it

We have left the age of sales and are now in the age of social. The way you market today is not by hard sell but by relationship. Even if you're putting together sales copy, you have to think about how it offers value to the potential reader.

What isn't valuable is a string of tweets that are little more than "buy my stuff" or "please RT this" messages. Some authors think it's a numbers game and repeating these messages will work over time.

They won't. They'll annoy more people than they'll attract.

5. It is first, and always, about the book

I don't care if you can out-promote and out-market anyone on the internet.

I don't care if you can afford to spend $100,000 to place ads for your books.

If your book fails to catch on with readers or, worse, turns them off, you're not going to do well over the long haul.

Which is how it should be, after all. The quality of the writing itself should be the main thing in this whole crazy process.

So you should concentrate a good chunk of your time, even more than you do on marketing, on a writing self-improvement program alongside your actual writing output.

Now is the best time in history to be a writer. No question about it. The barriers to entry have been destroyed and opportunities to generate income have taken their place. But you have to think strategically. Mark Coker, CEO of Smashwords, puts it this way: "The biggest challenge faced by self-published authors, it's not marketing, it's not discoverability, it's adopting the best practices of the very best publishers. It's about becoming a professional publisher."

Of course, if you have trouble with that, you can always partner with your cat Jingles.

How to Eat the Publishing Elephant

The elephant is a wonderful metaphorical animal.

We sometimes refer to the big issue everyone knows is there (but no one is talking about) as "the elephant in the room." Back in November of 2008, in conference rooms at publishing houses throughout New York, the elephant in the room was the Amazon Kindle. Was this device going to change publishing as we know it? Maybe no one wanted to talk about it back then, until the elephant broke out of the room and started stampeding all over midtown Manhattan.

Then there's the story of the three blind men coming up to an elephant. One touches the tail, another the leg, the other the trunk. Each man assumes the elephant is something other than it is, because he has only one bit of data. This we can liken to those who think they know everything there is about publishing (or anything, for that matter) when they only have experience with one part of it.

But the metaphor I want to work with today is the question, How do you eat an elephant? The answer, of course, is "one bite at a time."

This applies to the world of successful self-publishing. Note the key word *successful*. It's easy to self-publish (too easy, some would say). But to be successful at it is an entirely different matter.

A lot of people are expecting to eat the whole elephant in one bite. That's because some of the early adopters did that. Joe Konrath, Amanda Hocking, John Locke, Blake Crouch—these are some of the names that jumped in early and did some heavy munching. Barry Eisler famously walked away from a traditional print deal and went E to feast on elephant. Bob Mayer, king of the backlist, consumed several elephants early on when releasing all those titles close to one another.

But these are the notable exceptions to what is now the undeniable rule: The vast majority of writers will not get anywhere near *rapid* success. And if they expect to, they will be sorely disappointed and may even chuck the whole publishing thing.

Which is fine. We need less content, not more, because most of the two million self-published offerings out there are, well, pretty much in accord with Sturgeon's Law (you can look that one up).

But if you want to be successful as an indie author, you can be—if you eat the elephant one bite at a time and chew thoroughly.

By "success" I mean making a profit. You can make a profit from your self-publishing if you do certain things and do them right. (Like knowing how to write. That really helps.) How large a profit it is impossible to say up front. It may just be Starbucks money. Everyone's mileage is going to vary. But here's the rub: If you keep taking more and more bites, and do so carefully and with purpose, you have a chance to make more profit. That's called "business." If you want to be a professional writer, you are essentially running a small enterprise. Your job: provide value.

So here is some elephant wisdom that has become evident over this last crazy year of indie publishing: If you want to be successful at it *you need to be in it for the long haul, and by that I mean the rest of your life.*

Let me repeat: *the rest of your life.*

If you are truly a writer, that won't be difficult for you. But if you are just in this to try to make some easy lettuce, it will be. And should be.

A real writer writes, wants to write, would do it even if the prospect of making killer money was nil. Storytellers tell stories, which is why I plan to be found dead at my computer, my stone cold fingers over the keyboard. I only hope I have just typed "The End." Or better yet, "Upload."

I will keep on biting the elephant. And when I'm old and toothless, I'll *gum* the elephant. Because a real writer never stops.

Happy eating, friends.

A New Definition of Writing Success

"Rich are the records . . . with stories of penniless authors, who, sick with hope so long deferred, and at last despairing, have resorted to wild and tragic devices . . ."

So begins a story in the *Los Angeles Examiner,* New Year's Eve edition, December 31, 1905. The feature tells the tale of one such desperate author, a school teacher named Edith Allonby. For four years she'd labored on a novel, *The Fulfilment* [spelled with one "l"] into which she poured heart and soul. She had been published before, but her books had not been hits. *The Fulfilment* was going to change all that. In fact, Miss Allonby was certain its spiritual themes would change the world. (Indeed, she thought the book had been given to her by God, so the pressure was on.)

But the book was rejected. First, by her own publisher. Then by all the other publishing houses she sent it to. "I have submitted my book to all these men," she wrote in a note. "I have tried in vain. They will not accept it, yet shall 'The Fulfilment' reach the people to whom I appeal, for I have found another way."

After finishing the note, Miss Allonby changed into a silk evening gown, put fresh flowers in her hair, and sat in a comfortable chair. She was found dead the next day, her manuscript on her lap and an empty bottle of carbolic acid at her side.

And so it has been for countless authors for hundreds of years. Not normally ending in suicide (though such cases exist) but often in frustration, depression and despair. (*The Fulfilment*, BTW, was published in a limited edition after Miss Allonby's death.)

There was one primary reason for all this distress: *Their fate as writers was not in their own hands.* To get anywhere close to "success" they had to be accepted by an established publishing house (which alone had the means to produce and distribute a book), and then hope that they earned some money for their efforts.

Those two things—acceptance and income—defined writing success.

Included under "Getting Published," we can list some ancillary things writers hope for. Like getting on a bestseller list. Perhaps being nominated (even winning) a prestigious award. Maybe just the feeling of being part of an exclusive club.

But now we are experiencing a sea change on the "Income" side. We all know the traditional model is shrinking. Advances on new contracts are at historic lows. With physical shelf space disappearing, print revenues are down. And while digital income is up for the publishers, the slice of that pie given to authors remains stagnated at 25% of net (or roughly 17.5% of retail).

Still, many writers remain focused on "Getting Published." It represents some sort of "validation" even though it could very well mean less income and fewer readers.

But now a new model of writing success has appeared. Writers, for the first time since the troubadour era (when you could go out on your own and make up stories in song and take in some coin), have it within their power to get their writing out there without a middleman (the fancy term is "disintermediation").

And further, unlike self-published authors of yore, they actually have a chance to make real dough. Every day we are hearing more accounts of self-published writers who are earning significant income as independents.

Freedom is the invaluable commodity here. To be able to write what you truly want to write, and know that you can get it into the marketplace, is tremendously liberating. It is, in fact, the engine of happiness for a writer. It's exhilarating to write for yourself, see what you've written, fix it, and keep on writing—and be assured that it will have a place in the stream of commerce, for as long as you live.

This does not mean that going the traditional route is a spurious view of "success." If one seeks that validation, it's there to be pursued. The point is, however, that it is no longer the *only* game in town. Which is why I am more jazzed about being a writer than ever. Not just because of increased production and income, but because of the freedom to take responsibility for my own work.

Let me be quick to point out, however, that this responsibility carries challenges. Being in charge means you are CEO of your own company. You alone are in charge of quality control and production. You can expect to experience the stresses and strains of running a small business. You will need new skills to handle them. These can be acquired, but only through effort and self-discipline.

But it's more than worth it to be holding the reins of your own writing and life. I love seeing something I've written and edited make its appearance within a matter of weeks. I love getting paid every month. I love this whole new world of possibilities for tellers of tales.

I think Miss Allonby would have loved it, too. Had she

been able to self-publish, she might have lived a long, full life. Maybe she'd have written many more books, grown a readership, and made some money, too.

I know this because, in one of life's ironic and poignant turns, *The Fulfilment* by Edith Allonby is now available as an e-book.

Have you thought about what success as a writer means to you? It's worth it to sit down and map out just how that would look. Then begin your journey toward that goal.

For Authors With Agents and Publishers

I have many professional novelist friends. As I began establishing a footprint in self-publishing, some have come to me with questions. One of the queries concerns what to do about self publishing when you have a traditional contract and an agent representing you.

For example, what happens if you broach the subject of putting out some self-published work and your agent reacts negatively? What about the editor at your publishing house? How should you handle these conversations?

I've broken down the advice into several issues.

1. Branding and investment by your publisher

Branding is not nearly so important in self-publishing,

though it's still a consideration for you to make. But for a publishing house using the old print/bookstore model, it is very important. A publisher who is investing in you obviously has an interest in protecting its investment, building you up for the future. They have images of you running wild on the internet like some latter day Isadora Duncan, eventually being strangled by a scarf of your own making. That's a true concern from the publisher's standpoint. It needs to be addressed by you in a professional manner. See below.

2. Agents

Agents are hurting just like traditional publishing is. Advances are down and they have to think long term about your future because it's their future, too. But getting angry should not be the reaction. That bespeaks a desire to cut off any and all such thinking on your part. But as a writer working today, with the changing landscape, you have the right — indeed, the responsibility — to be thinking about your own long term future.

It's dicey now, because it used to be you and your agent had only one objective — the traditional publishing world — and there was no conflict there. Everybody knew his or her respective roles.

Now we've added another possibility, i.e. real, substantial and in some cases huge income from self-publishing. Which puts the agent in an awkward position as to advising the client. How do you objectively advise someone to pursue work for which the agent will receive no commission?

3. Writing income

There is real money to be made in self-publishing. You have a right to go out and earn it. Your publisher has the right to protect its investment. These two things may come into conflict. Thus, you will have to make this assessment for the future: Can I make more, and be happier, long term, publishing my own work? Or am I happy where I am, working with a team, but most likely making less money over the years?

And understand that the publisher can decide not to renew its investment in you at any time. Even while you're still under contract, mind you. You might have a series that hasn't met expectations, and the next book you turn in may be left to die on the vine. That may mean another year or two where you're tied up, years you could have been earning income and growing a readership via self-publishing.

4. Pseudonymous publishing

This is of course an option, but presents a couple of major problems. You need publicity to sell books on your own. That takes massive amounts of time investment, which you have to make in *addition* to the marketing of books under your own name. You would essentially be starting from scratch in social media, etc., and running two platform building programs at the same time. This doesn't seem a wise use of time. (I am currently using a pseudonym with a traditionally published series, but openly and for brand distinction only. So I bootstrap off my already established profile.)

Further, it's impossible to be truly pseudonymous anymore. Eventually your agent and publisher will know what you're doing. If they have signed off on your doing this, however, no problem, except for the one mentioned above.

My advice is to first work with your publisher on the idea of you putting some truly non-competing and, indeed, complementary work out on your own, such as short stories or novellas. Just like in the "old days" when a novelist would supplement income by selling stories to a magazine, or some such. And then his name would get out there even more and that would generate publicity for his other work.

Publishers need to see this as you making new readers. That's why publishers put out free promotions sometimes on older works. They want to bump up your back and front list. This is the same principle, only now you are making some extra money.

In view of all the above, what should a writer do right now?

1. Write yourself a "white paper"

You ought to sit down and write out a vision document for yourself, with proposals of how you would like to proceed with your writing life. This will serve not only as a clarifying document for yourself, but also as an "educational paper" for your agent and/or publishing house. It will be as a starting point for professional discussion, so you need to think these issues through for yourself. Take time with this paper. Gather information from blogs and discussions that are already ongoing. Educate yourself, figure out who you want to be as a writer, not just now but ten years from now.

Stay rational. Don't fall for the anger trap, because there's a lot of that out there. Writers are dumping on the traditional publishing industry when they should simply be thinking about it without letting their anger distract them.

In the same way, no agent or editor should "go ballistic." If someone does that, they are not acting professionally, and you should take that into consideration for your future. You are in a business relationship with your these people, and should be treated that way.

2. Prepare for an E-future

The future is now, as they say, but it's going to be even more about digital content in the years ahead. The tsunami is bigger and faster than anyone thought it would be a couple of years ago.

You can prepare by thinking things through as if you didn't have a traditional publishing contract. What would you write if you had total freedom? How would you want to market yourself? What books or stories are you dying to write that you are not writing at the moment because of your traditional schedule?

You might even try writing some of those projects on spec, just for yourself. It doesn't mean you have to go out and publish them right away. But you can be laying a foundation for yourself, and be ready to move.

In my kickboxing exercise video, the cute little instructor constantly goes back to a "boxer's shuffle," and says, "You're ready for anything!" Writers today need to be in a boxer's shuffle, because it's a challenge out there and you don't want to get knocked out.

One thing more. The traditional publishing industry has gotten used to treating writers as powerless cogs in their commercial machine. If the cog help generate income, they're happy. But if they determine the cog does not generate enough return, they can take a wrench and remove the cog and throw it with a tinny clank into a dumpster. They understand there are enough writers willing to be cogs that they don't have to worry about any one cog.

But suddenly writers have more power to determine their own fate. This is causing a bit of cognitive (pun intended) dissonance in publishing houses, and even among agents. Things are not what they once were. How come all these cogs all of a sudden are building their own machines? And making money doing it? We were the only ones who were able to do that in publishing! Now what?

So I understand publishers and agents wondering about their futures, about their very existence. Well, welcome to the world of the writer. We've been worrying about those things our whole writing lives, because you, the traditional publishing industry, held all the power and could discard us at any time. The difference is that now we have leverage, power and alternatives. Sure, you're nervous. But let's all quit going ballistic and sit down and figure out the best thing for everyone. If best means an author goes one way and you go another, so be it.

Interview with JSB on Indie Publishing

– Tell us a little about your indie book or books, for readers who aren't familiar with your work.

I have great admiration for the old pulp writers, the guys who made a living pounding out stories during the Depression, some of whom became truly great. People like Hammett, Chandler, Cornell Woolrich. I like the idea of being prolific and being good at the same time. That's what I strive for.

With indie publishing, I can put out more work for my readers. I specialize in suspense. Last year I published two collections that each included a complete novella and three stories. I did the novellas in the style of James M. Cain, another prolific writer of the old school.

One More Lie is the title novella of one collection. It's the story of what happens when you make one bad choice and try to cover it with another.

Watch Your Back is the novella in the other collection, and it's one of those stories where the too-slick hero gets involved with a femme fatale. Sort of like *Double Indemnity*. Who is using whom? This collection also features a story readers seem to love, "Heed the Wife," with the sort of twist ending I love.

I find these types of stories to be profoundly moral. I think the best noir comes out of the view that rough justice happens. It's not pretty, but it gets the job done.

Also, I put out a collection of some of my articles on fiction writing as an e-book, *Writing Fiction for All You're Worth.* And I started a short story series, boxing tales set in 1950s Los Angeles.

All this was done as I completed work on my contracted books.

– You have several books published through traditional publishers — including a new writing book through Writer's Digest. What made you decide to self-publish some of your work? Do you plan to keep doing both, or are you leaning toward one over the other?

It's all about options and freedom, isn't it? So long as you are honoring your traditional contracts, and you have negotiated them in the proper way, and you're getting along with everybody, having an independent line that complements your traditional work is a no-brainer. It's real income, and I have this quaint notion that writers are entitled to earn real income from what they write.

Of course, things are a little dicey right now because many authors with traditional contracts are running into their non-compete clauses, and some publishers are playing hardball with them. That's fodder for another discussion.

But going forward, writers and agents have to be wise, creative and stalwart in their negotiating with traditional publishers. And publishers need to realize that author good will is something they're going to need long term.

– How do you think your traditional publishing experience affected your indie publishing experience?

Because I wrote my way up through the traditional channel, over the course of twenty years, I had the chance to work with some great editors. I got better as a writer doing all the hard work of meeting deadlines and editorial comments. This is invaluable. For those who are going right into independent publishing, I urge them to find ways to make it hard on themselves. Study the craft diligently, get hammered by freelance editors or critique partners or beta readers. Don't assume that this thing is easy.

I've also gotten to know the publishing industry well, how publishers think. I apply that to my own independent publishing. I try to stay objective about my own work and plan several years in advance.

– With traditional publishing, the publisher provides the editor. How did you find one for the work you published? What tips would you offer for others who are looking for an editor?

You don't just want to pick someone out of the Yellow Pages or Google. The best way is through trusted companies, like Writer's Digest and their 2d Draft service, or recommendations from other writers. How do you find people to make those recommendations? Go to writers conferences. That's one of the best things a new author can do. Go and network, meet editors and fellow writers and ask questions. Do research, find people who have good reputations. When you find somebody you really work well with, it's gold. Nurture that relationship.

– What steps did you take before publishing to get feedback on the quality of the story?

My usual MO is this: I write a first draft, let it sit for a time, come back to it and edit it myself. I give that next draft to my wife, who is a terrific editor and proofreader. I take her notes and incorporate them. If this is a project with my agent, he gets the next crack at it.

If it's an indie project, I have a network of beta readers who are generous and good at what they do. I have them go over it, make additional changes, and then finally go out to a copy editor. This is something I pay for and it is money well spent.

– What were the biggest surprises you had before indie publication? After?

The biggest surprise, to me, was how fast the digital revolution was moving a year-and-a-half ago. We all knew digital would take more and more territory, but the speed of the change was amazing, especially after Christmas 2010. That's when my wife gave me a Kindle. I am a book lover. I love my collection of paperback originals from the 1950s and hardcovers from favorite authors. I never thought I would truly lose the desire to hold a physical book in my hands.

But the e-readers like the Kindle are wonderful, amazing devices. I got hooked on mine and knew millions more would, too, and very soon.

That's when I decided to jump in with some indie books of my own. I had no idea what to expect in terms of sales. But the first couple of months were a pleasant surprise. It showed me what the possibilities really are. I don't see most writers hitting grand slams the first time out. Or maybe ever. But if you create volume and can deliver the goods, you have a good chance of making a fair income over the course of time. These are a lot better odds than the overwhelming majority of writers in history have ever had.

– What's been the most challenging part of the process? Is that different from your experience with traditional publishing?

The most challenging part is internal quality control. With traditional publishing, you're working with a team of professionals and a window of time of a year to eighteen months per book. One of the most exciting things about indie publishing is the speed with which you can bring out books. But you have to find ways to give your work the attention it needs, everything from cover design to marketing copy to editing and formatting. You simply have to think like a business for all these tasks.

– What advice would you offer for currently unpublished writers considering the indie route? How about for traditionally published authors considering switching?

For any writer considering self-publishing, I urge them not to move too fast. That may seem contradictory to what I said above, but remember I've been a professional writer for two decades. And for several years before that I was diligently learning how to tell a story, how to plot, how to write a book that moved. If you don't know these things it doesn't matter how fast you publish, nobody is going to continue to read your work. There's an old sports saying: "It's not the will to win that counts. It's the will to prepare to win." Everybody wants to publish and make money. But how many are willing to pay the price to become good enough writers to make that money?

If a traditionally published writer is happy with a publishing house, I'd say find ways to work with that house so you can put out complementary material. Writers and agents have to help publishing houses to see that this can be a win–win. The indie work can make new readers for the traditionally published work. Unfortunately, that kind of thinking is in short supply right now. Everything is moving too fast and publishers are naturally concerned about the future. I would say to the traditionalist and his or her agent, get very clear about contracts, and what you are willing to walk away from.

– Is there any indie "conventional wisdom" you disagree with? Why?

Perhaps the idea that you have to be a monster marketer and self-promoter. I actually think marketing and promotion and social media, while important, are going to be less so in the future. That's because there is so much of it—a constant daily onslaught—that no one, and I mean no one, is going to dominate the marketing stream.

The only thing that's going to work over time is a steady production of quality material, which will lead to reader recommendations and word-of-mouth. Your marketing and social media can get you an introduction, but it's your work that is going to have to carry the day. And that is exactly how it should be.

– The big discussion point lately has been KDP Select and Amazon's demand for exclusivity in exchange for participation. What are your thoughts on the tradeoffs?

It's a simple business decision, nothing more, nothing less. Amazon is a business. A HUGE business. And they are making this offer that is in their long-term interest. That's what businesses DO.

They are offering the chance for indie authors to make their work available for free for a period of time, and also a share of a pool of moolah based upon the lending program for their Prime members.

So, you sit down and ask if it's in your interest to accept that offer. I am doing Select with a couple of my stories, and so far I like the results vis-à-vis the free downloads. This was the main reason I did it. I think the downstream effect—that is, making new readers—is in my financial interest, regardless of what comes in from the lending fund.

– One of the challenges for indie authors has been the large volume of work out there that isn't ready for publication, especially since readers have limited tools to search through the pile for the quality books. Do you think this will always be a problem, or is it just a phase in the evolution of e-publishing?

We will always be subject to Sturgeon's Law, which states that 90% of everything is crap. That's not going to change. So readers will find various ways to deal with that. Free sampling perhaps, or trusted web hubs. But I don't think there is ever going to be one dominant location to find quality work. The marketplace is too vast now, and everyone can get a seat at the table. So success will happen this way: a reader will love a book or story and want to buy more from that author. If the author has more to sell, he or she will make more bank.

It's as simple and as profound as that. The best thing to do is to write crazy good books and stories and get them out into the market. And keep doing that, over and over, for the rest of your life.

Further Thoughts on Indie Publishing

You're a successful author who's sold a lot of books, but in support of the writing career you speak and teach at conferences, tweet, blog, give interviews. What myth would you most like to dispel for new writers about the successful writer's life?

That it ever gets easier. In fact, in some ways, it gets

harder. Or should. Your standards go up with each book. You know more, you set the bar higher. And you want it to, if you're a real writer. I have a number of bestselling author friends, and they all feel this way. It's nice to have a career doing this, certainly. But it's work, too. Don't think it's ever a fluffy ride on a cloud.

You've stated elsewhere that new writers need to focus on craft first — without a good book the rest doesn't matter. But, at what point in an author's early career should they begin thinking about the business behind the writing? How does one plan for that? What are the key items to think through, and consider?

A writer should think about this being a business from the very start. Know how the business runs, what publishers and agents and readers look for, what sells and does not sell. Learn how to plan at least two years ahead. Set goals for finishing projects and getting them out there. Learn about production — editing, cover design, copywriting and copyrighting. This approach establishes its own momentum. You can be doing things every day toward your goals, and there's a power in that.

At the same time, never think that business knowledge and marketing can cover a multitude of writing sins. One still has to be able to consistently deliver the goods, and that means learning the craft by writing, revising, studying, getting feedback, and more writing.

You have a wide range of new "products" being offered through e-books, traditionally published fiction and non-fiction books (at my count you released 9 books in different formats on Amazon in 2011). There's been a lot of doom and gloom talk about publishing lately. In your opinion, is this a good time to be a new writer/author?

Never a better time to be an author! Ever. Period. Because of choices. It's always been hard to get published traditionally. And yes, it's harder at this moment because of the shakeups in the industry. Not impossible. New authors are getting deals. But we have the independent route now that means there's a real alternative. There wasn't before. Yes, you could pay a lot of money to self-publish in print, but 99% of the time you couldn't sell enough to make any real dough. Not only has indie publishing been a boon for books, but also for short stories and novellas. The latter market was virtually non-existent. Now it's back, better than ever.

Yes, it's a great time to be a writer.

A lot of indie authors are telling new writers they must be prolific and produce new content often, 3-5 books a year, to be successful. Not many traditionally published authors can manage that kind of output. Looking ahead, what do you predict will be the key factors for a successful writing career? Being prolific? A wide range of "products"? Social media clout?

I love being prolific, but I don't think you need to put a number on the speed of production. Consistency is a better word. A writer who wants to succeed at this needs to establish a consistent rate of production (I always use a weekly quota of words), and plan projects out in advance (I have enough for at least five years hence). The "keys" to success are quality and consistency, which is why I advocate a systematic studying of the craft of writing for the rest of your life. Some writers sniff at craft study, but they are fooling themselves and others. Would you want your brain operated on by a surgeon who doesn't keep up with the medical journals? Make craft study a part of the "quality control" of your business — and all writers are in business for themselves.

Social media certainly has a role to play, but if one gets obsessive about it, the ROE (Return on Energy) just doesn't add up. Recent studies have shown that books are not sold in great numbers via social media. Create relationships with readers in social media, but always remember the best thing to do is write excellent books and let word of mouth take over. Concentrate your energy there.

Any advice for emerging authors about the business of writing?

Learn business principles: goal setting, time management, marketing fundamentals, quality control, pricing, copywriting, sales. You can get good books on all of these and study them when you can.

The most important things a writer can do are, in order of importance:

1. Write

2. Keep improving what you write (study craft, get critiques)

3. Sell what you write (via marketing and business principles)

And try to enjoy the ride.

Bonus Section: Conflict & Suspense Strategies Illustrated

What follows is a conflict and suspense analysis of sections from my novel, *No Legal Grounds* (Zondervan, 2007). Since I wrote it, it gives me an opportunity to show you what I was thinking and let you see how it worked out in actual practice.

I'll be showing examples of:

1. Getting the idea
2. Opening disturbance
3. Doorway of No Return #1
4. Interruptions
5. Conflict among allies
6. End of scene prompt
7. Inner conflict
8. Tense dialogue
9. Emotional cliffhanger

10. Scene structure (objective, obstacle, outcome)
11. Raising the stakes
12. Doorway of No Return #2
13. Stretching the tension
14. Cut away technique

The Idea

I got the idea for the novel the following way: Someone from my college years contacted me via email, and wanted to meet with me. He wouldn't say why. I responded with a slight brush off, then got a second email that was insistent. Then another one after that even more pushy. I finally consented to a meeting, which led to me being given the hard sell.

Naturally, I was thinking "What if . . ." during all this time. There was natural conflict here.

Which led to my "borrowing" an old plot. One of my favorite John D. MacDonald books is *The Executioners*, which became the basis of the movie *Cape Fear*. In the original, Robert Mitchum plays a creep named Max Cady, who was prosecuted by lawyer Sam Bowden (Gregory Peck). Cady gets out of prison and comes to Sam's town to stalk him and his family. There's nothing the law can do so long as Cady doesn't try anything overt.

That was it. I wanted to do my own version of that central conflict, but changing the motivations and plot developments.

I kept the name *Sam* as an homage to the MacDonald

novel.

Here is how it begins:

1.

Hey buddy! Long time! Tracked you down after reading your blurb on the Prominent Alumni page. Prominent! You made it, buddy. I always knew you would, though it was all pretty crazy back there freshman year. Remember that? Wild times, oh yes. How'd we ever make it out of the dorm!

So I found your law firm website and then you and here I am! I'm in town! We have a lot of catching up to do. Call me, man. Can't wait to see you.

Sam Trask vaguely remembered the name at the end of the e-mail. You remember guys named Nicky, even if you don't think about them for twenty-five years.

Nicky Oberlin. That's how he'd signed the e-mail, along with a phone number.

The tightness in his chest, the clenching he'd been feeling for the last few weeks, returned. Why should that happen because of one random e-mail? Because it presented a complication, *a thing that called for response.* He did not need that now, not with the way things were at home.

Sam took a deep breath, leaned back in his chair in his Beverly Hills office, and tried to relax. Didn't happen. He kept seeing his daughter's face in his computer monitor, screaming at him.

A quick knock on his door bumped Sam from his thoughts. Lew poked his head in. "A minute?"

Opening Disturbance

The opening disturbance does not have to be a major upset in the character's life. It can be anything that causes a ripple in the ordinary world.

Here, my character's ordinary world is a law firm, where he is well established. And, a little later, his home and family.

The disturbance is an e-mail that he receives after being "tracked down" by some old college acquaintance he does not even remember.

Interruption

Before Sam can think more about the e-mail, he is interrupted by his law partner. The scene continues.

Sam motioned him in. Lew Newman was Sam's age, forty-seven, and wore his sandy hair short, which gave his sharp nose and alert eyes added prominence. When Lew was with the Brooklyn D.A.'s office he was known as The Hawk, and Sam could see why. He would've hated to be a witness about to pecked by The Hawk's cross-examination. He was glad they were partners and not adversaries.

"We're going into high gear against the good old U. S. of A. this week," Lew said.

Sam nodded. "Got it on the radar." The FulCo case was by far the biggest Newman & Trask had ever handled. Potentially a billion at stake. That thought gave Sam's chest another quick squeeze.

"Cleared everything else?" Lew said.

"One matter to take care of."

"What's that?"

"Harper."

Lew rolled his eyes. "Sam, I'm all for doing a little of this stuff, but not to the exclusion of the bread and butter."

"I'll take care of it."

"Please do."

"I said I would, okay?"

Lew put his hands up. "Just asking. I get to ask, don't I?"

"Of course. Sorry."

"Need you, buddy. I know things haven't been the best with—"

"I can handle it, Lew."

His partner nodded. "How's Heather doing, anyway?"

Sam did not want to talk about his daughter, not now. "We're working on it."

"Good. She'll pull through. She's a good kid."

Sam said nothing.

"So on Harper—"

"Lew, please—"

"Let me just say this once, okay? We do have a business to run, and—"

"You want me to get rid of the Harper file ASAP."

"That would be nice. Can you settle it?"

"Not right away."

"Why not?"

"I need more discovery, or it'll be undervalued."

"Come on, Sam. What about your value to the shop?"

Always with the cost-benefit analysis, Lew was. Maybe that was what really had changed for Sam in the last four years. When he'd converted, a little of the drive for the dollar had gone from his life.

As if sensing he'd stuck a foot over the line, Lew said, "Look, I trust your judgment, of course. But a quick settlement surely is going to be within the ballpark, give or take, and what's the problem with that?"

"No problem at all. Girl goes blind, we can toss her a few bones and move on."

"Come on, I don't mean that. Just think about it for me, will you? Harper off the table. I love you, sweetie." He made a golfing motion. "How about eighteen next week?"

Golf was always the way Lew made up. "Sure."

"I love you more," Lew said, and left.

Conflict among allies

Lew and Sam are on the "same side." They're law partners. But even dialogue between allies needs to have some conflict. So we have a disagreement over how to handle a particular case.

For a long time Sam swiveled in his chair, as if the motion would gently rock his thoughts into some cohesive order. But it wasn't happening, because Sarah Harper was not a case he wanted to expedite.

The tightness came back. Come on, he scolded himself. No heart attack. You're not even fifty years old yet. Guys like you don't die before fifty. He kept in shape, ran three miles every other day, didn't have too many extra pounds. But he knew there was no guarantee. One of his old friends from UCLA Law had just gone to the cooling rack playing pickup basketball.

One minute Tom had been a hard charging partner at O'Melveny, and boom, the next he's an obit in *California Lawyer*. It could happen to anyone.

Sam rubbed his chest and looked back at the monitor. *Nicky Oberlin*. He tried to remember the face that went with the name. Didn't come to him.

Truth was, a lot of that first year at U. C. Santa Barbara up the coast was lost in a brain fog. He was still a long way off from a sober life then, and most of what he remembered of freshman year was a dorm known for grass and beer and late night parties.

So this blast from the past was hearkening back to days he'd just as soon forget.

Was he the guy who came into his dorm room one night, hammered to the gills, and tried to roll out Sam's bed—while Sam was still in it? A lot of crazy things happened back then. It was a wonder any of them passed their classes.

Yeah, that might have been Nicky, a little guy with a moustache. But then again . . . brain fog.

And in the fog, like the trill of night bird, a faint vibration of unease. Oberlin had sent this to Sam's private e-mail address. It wasn't supposed to be readily available. It would have taken some doing to find it. Apparently, Oberlin had. Which bothered him no end. It was like . . . an intrusion, and by a guy he really didn't know.

He closed his eyes for a moment and expressed his favorite prayer of late, for wisdom. Having a seventeen-year-old daughter who seemed determined to throw her life down the toilet necessitated divine intervention on an almost daily basis.

Now, he needed wisdom for his professional life. The Harper family had come to him in their hour of greatest need. He would not drop the ball.

His chest clenched and he took in as much air as he could. This was not what he thought life would be at this point in his career. He thought he'd be at the pinnacle of his profession, able to coast along at a hardworking but smooth pace, with his wife and kids along for the ride.

Instead, he was tighter than hangman's rope, and wondering if the American dream, as it were, was imploding in on him.

He didn't need any more tasks or obligations, no matter how small. With a touch of his index finger, he deleted Nicky Oberlin's e-mail.

He hoped Nicky wouldn't take offense.

End of scene prompt

Sam hopes Nicky won't "take offense." Which leaves that distinct possibility open. End scene.

Sam goes home after work, and meets his wife. They are a happy couple in general, but I always want to avoid Happy People in Happy Land syndrome. It's possible to find tension in every exchange, so the scene starts this way:

"Don't worry, I'm not going to be one of *those* kind of wives, complaining up and down how much time her husband spends at the office."

Sam took a root beer from the refrigerator, turned to face his wife. "But a little complaining every now and again never hurt, right?"

"Is that what you think I do?"

"Not in so many words, but lately . . ."

"Lately what?" She put her hands on her hips.

Uh-oh. Sam called that the Gesture, but not to Linda's face. The Gesture always raised his macho hackles. His wife was smart and insightful, and she could usually see through him. Drove him crazy sometimes. And when she was angry, and her hazel eyes caught the light, they sparked like flint on stone.

"Hints," he said. "You drop hints."

"What, would you rather I hit you right between the eyes?"

"Maybe a little more directness *would* be a good thing."

"Maybe I don't want to add to your stress, okay? Did you ever think of it that way?"

"Of course." He stepped over to her to kiss her. She gave him her cheek. "Don't pout," he said.

"When you deserve the lips again, you'll get them."

Now the conversation turns toward dinner, but then quickly gets to their daughter, Heather. Notice the **interruptions** in the dialogue:

"So what about a steak? You want me to do up a nice steak dinner?" They were happy meat eaters, and Sam considered himself master of the barbeque.

"Oh yeah," Linda said.

"How many?"

"Three. Max, you, and me."

"Where's Heather?"

Linda paused. "She's out."

"With who?"

"Let's not."

Dead giveaway. "Not that Roz girl."

"Sam, I know —"

"I thought we told her —"

"Sam, please. We've been through it with her and it just leads to more anger."

Indeed, his circuits were charged. They sizzled with a high current whenever the subject of Heather's associations came up. "Who's in control around here? I don't want her seeing that girl."

The argument continues. I wanted to stretch it out while dropping in more exposition. Remember, confrontational dialogue is a way to give the reader information without stopping for an information dump.

"Heather is seventeen and pigheaded, like someone else I know."

She said it in a lighthearted way, but Sam wasn't into being light at the moment. "What if she wanted to go out with a serial killer?"

"Sam, Roz is hardly a serial killer."

"She's trouble, is what she is."

"That's a little harsh."

"Is it? I saw her at Starbucks one day, hanging out with a bunch of lowlifes."

"How did you know they were lowlifes?"

"Come on."

"What happened to the presumption of innocence?"

He ignored the dig. "Where do they go, these two? They go to concerts—who knows what kind of music these bands are playing. The lyrics. Have you heard some of the lyrics out there?"

"You know who you sound like?"

"Who?"

"Our parents."

"That's depressing." Sam went to the living room and plopped on the sofa.

"Don't pick up the remote," Linda said.

He picked up the remote.

Inner conflict

In the following exchange, Sam is in negotiations with a big time lawyer for an insurance company. The case is the one Sam's partner alluded to earlier. It involves a Bronze Medal winning Olympic figure skater, Sarah Harper, who went blind due to a negligent diagnosis from a doctor. Sam has become emotionally invested in the case, so I wanted to show what he was up against. Should he risk Sarah not getting anything by going to trial against a lawyer who hasn't lost a case in fifteen years? Or take the safe route but with a low settlement number?

"Not bad," Cohen said, slipping out of his coat and placing it on an ornate wooden rack inside his office door.

Cohen sat behind his desk, his chair slightly elevated so he could look down on whomever he faced.

"Why don't you come work for me?" Cohen smiled, gestured toward the grand view outside the window. "I can offer you all this."

Sam resisted the urge to say *Away from me, Satan!* and merely nodded. "Thanks for the offer, but I'm happy where I am."

"In a two-man boutique? You could do so much better. And by the way, I wouldn't make this offer to your partner."

Sam said nothing, preferring to let Cohen get over his blather so they could get down to business. Still, a small part of him wondered what Cohen meant.

"I mean," Cohen said, "you're the quiet, smart one. Not a hothead. Hotheads get a lot of publicity, but they end up burning themselves. And their clients. I'm not joking about the offer."

"No thanks, Larry."

"Idealist, are you? Clinging to the myth of the underdog versus the big, bad insurance company?"

"Maybe we should get to the offer."

Cohen nodded. "Sure. I'm offering not to go to trial and leave your client with a big fat nothing."

A negotiating ploy, Cohen playing off his well-deserved reputation as one of the most successful insurance defense lawyers the country had ever seen. Sam knew he had to take that detail into consideration.

Sam waited silently for the offer.

"Nine hundred," Cohen said.

The nerve endings inside Sam's chest started vibrating. "That's way too low," he said.

"It's what I've come up with." Not giving an inch.

"I'll give you time to reconsider."

Cohen leaned forward, hovering over his desk. "You don't quite get it, do you? I've been doing this for thirty-five years, you think I'm bluffing? It's all about information, Sam, you know that. I know about you and your partner. I know you have bigger fish to fry, that a trial would distract you from that. And I know this case inside and out, and I know how to win trials. You really want to take that risk?"

In his mind's eye, Sam saw Sarah Harper, blind, shaking her head in court, wondering why the jury had returned with a verdict against her claim.

"I'll give you twenty-four hours to discuss it with your

client and get back to me," Cohen said. "After that, no more offers. We go to court."

As Sam drives away in his car the inner conflict is experienced on the page. This is one of the best ways to get your reader bonded to a Lead character.

He hated bullies, and Cohen was the classic bully of the litigator type. He had the deep pockets behind him and could throw his weight around all he wanted. Didn't matter what justice demanded.

Problem was, Cohen had the trial skills to back it all up.

Sam tuned the radio to smooth jazz and took a couple of deep breaths. Rationally, he knew he had only two options.

He could convince the Harpers that the insurance company's offer was the best they were likely to get. They wouldn't be pleased, but Lew would be. He could put this one behind him and get on to bigger and better things.

Bigger? Better? And what was Sarah Harper? Canned ham?

But Larry Cohen truly was formidable. To go through all the time and effort of a trial and come out empty would be worse than settling for what amounted to chump change from a huge insurance company.

Was he afraid to go up against Cohen? Maybe a little. But he could overcome that, he was certain. Once the trial juices started flowing, he'd be all right.

What to do?

Take it to the Harpers. Just lay it out for them and see what they say. Maybe they'd jump at it.

Nicky e-mails again, indicating that he can "help" Sam on one of his cases. To get him off his back Sam consents to meeting him at Starbucks, hoping that will finally put an end to things.

Tuesday morning, Sam walked into Starbucks and saw a man immediately sit up, smile, and wave.

Sam did not recognize him, but it was clear he recognized Sam.

"Nicky?"

He stood and shook Sam's hand. "You look great, man."

"It's all an illusion."

Nicky was short, a little thick around the waist, and had an advanced case of male pattern baldness. His features were orbical—round eyes, round nose, round cheekbones. He wore a white golf shirt that stretched over his belly before tucking away in his tan slacks.

"No, I mean it," Nicky said, giving Sam's form an admiring glance. "You have to work out."

"I run."

"Gotta do the same." Nicky patted his stomach. "The all-beer diet is a fraud."

"I figured that one out a long time ago."

"Only martinis and scotch for you, I bet."

The dialogue starts out as typical friendly banter. I didn't want that to go on too long. I wanted to start to build it to being uncomfortable for Sam. The crack about "martinis and scotch" seems to be a subtle jab of envy. The conversation continues with Nicky prodding Sam about his personal life, until Sam finally asks about Nicky. The dialogue gets more uncomfortable. Notice the interruptions.

"What about you, Nicky? You indicated there was a way

you could help me."

"Right, right."

"You mentioned a case. What was that all about?"

"Your case, Sam."

"I have several cases —"

"The ice skater." Nicky raised his eyebrows.

"May I ask how you know about that?"

"Internet, dude. How I found you in the first place."

"What, you did some background on me?"

"Oh, easy stuff. Wanted to see how well you were doing. Making UCSB proud!"

Sam forced a chuckle. "So what did you mean by help?"

"You know, maybe research or something like that. I'm a cyber king, dude. I'd love to give you a hand."

"Well, that's real nice of you to offer, but we have paralegals to —"

"I'm not talking about normal channels, Sam. I can dig into places you've missed. Let me show you."

And open up a can of trouble. Wouldn't it be great to have

Larry Cohen find out someone was rooting around in *places you've missed.*

"Thanks," Sam said, "but—"

"No thanks? I got it." Nicky sat back in his chair.

"It's not that I don't appreciate—"

"You have a card, Sam?"

Sam hesitated. Then he fished a card out of his wallet and gave it to Nicky.

"Very slick," Nicky said. "Raised letters and everything."

"Makes us seem more important than we are."

"Yeah," Nicky said, "that's what lots of people think."

A tick of unease hit Sam. He looked at his watch. "Hey, Nicky, I hate to say, but I've got to run."

"So soon?"

"I'm sorry. Lawyering." He stood. "Everybody wants a piece of me. It was sure great to see you, Nicky."

Nicky stood up and put out his hand. "Let's do this again."

"Sure." Sam shook Nicky's hand, hoping Nicky would pick up on the noncommittal tone in his voice.

Nicky held the grip. "I mean it."

"Right. Bye, Nicky."

Nicky slipped Sam's card into his shirt pocket. "We'll be in touch," he said.

Doorway of No Return #1

Sam has a heart-wrenching scene with his client and her parents, about the lowball settlement offer, and a blowup with his daughter, and another tense scene with Lew, his law partner. Nicky Oberlin tries another jovial email that Sam ignores. With all this going on, Sam takes a call at his office. It's Nicky. As Sam tries to get rid of him, Nicky won't be gotten rid of as the scene builds to a shocking end. After this, it will be a matter of psychological death, because his family is going to be stalked. Sam's objective is to *get away from* Nicky.

Sam knew who it was. He went to his office, picked up and heard the jovial tones of Nicky Oberlin.

"Hey, I didn't hear back from you. Thought I'd give you a call, see if everything's alright."

Sam didn't want to do this little phone dance. "Everything's fine, Nicky."

"Then when are we getting together?"

"I don't know if that's going to happen. I just found out I'm going to be extremely busy for the foreseeable future. Not really going to have time."

"Time for old friends?"

"Time for a lot of things. But I've got your card and —"

"Hey, sounds like you're giving your old buddy the brush."

"It's not that."

"I think it is."

Now what? He really *was* giving Nicky the brush-off, and it was patently obvious.

"Nicky, let me just put it this way: I really appreciate the fact that you looked me up after all these years, that you wanted to get together and all that, but right now I just don't have time to fit in any new social relationships. I've got family things going on and law things going on, you know how it is. So let's just leave it at that, and remember the old times."

Pause. "You mean we'll always have Paris?"

"What was that?"

"You know, that line from *Casablanca*? Bogart says it to

Bergman just before he dumps her on the plane."

"Oh yeah. Right."

"Well sorry, Sam. I'm not getting on the plane."

Sam's chest tightened a little. "Excuse me?"

"No brush-off."

"I don't know what you're talking about, Nicky, but—"

"Then let me make it real clear, boss. You and I are not through seeing each other. We're college chums. I didn't hold much sway in the dorms, if you'll recall. Nobody wanted to room with me, remember? I was the only guy in the dorm with a single. Not that I minded, considering all the jerks we had."

Things were starting to get seriously bent. Sam considered just hanging up but figured that would only lead to more calls, more e-mails. He had to settle this now.

"I don't choose to see you, Nicky, okay? That's that."

"You didn't hear me, did you, boss? You really didn't hear me. See, that's been your problem all along. You didn't hear me back in the old dorm, either. You were into yourself. You still are."

"I'm going to say good-bye now, Nicky. I wish you well, I—"

"Linda okay with that?"

"What?"

"Linda. Your wife, remember? And Heather, and little Max?"

Sam sat up ramrod straight in his chair. "You tell me exactly what you're saying."

"A fine Christian family, right Sam? Pillars of the community and all that."

"Listen—"

"You listen. What would it do to your little family unit if they found out about that thing? That little item from back at the old alma mater? I bet you haven't told Linda about it."

"There's nothing to tell."

"I think there is."

"I'm hanging up." But he held for just a second more.

"I'm talking about your child, Sam. The one your girlfriend had. The one who's alive and well and living in good old Southern California. Did you tell Linda about the kid, Sam?"

Sam was speechless, numb.

"I didn't think so," Nicky Oberlin said.

Emotional cliffhanger

After Nicky's line, above, I cut away to a scene involving Sam's daughter. The reader naturally wants to know more about this child and the new threat Nicky represents.

A scene with objective, obstacles, outcome

In this scene, Nicky has shown up at a Little League game with Sam's son, Max, playing. He stands near the field, yelling fake encouragement at Max. Sam's objective is to get Nicky out of there before he makes Max too distracted. The obstacle is Nicky himself armed with a knowledge of the law. The outcome is a setback to Sam.

"Get out of here," Sam said.

Nicky kept looking at the field. "Be ready to go, Maxie."

Sam reached out to Nicky's shoulder and spun him. "I said get out!"

Nicky looked at him with a half smile. "Hey, I'm trying to watch a game here."

"You're a sick man. I don't want you around me or my family, understand?"

"A guy can't come to a baseball game in America anymore?"

"Not the way you're doing it. This has just become a police matter."

"Cops?"

"That's what I said, unless you —"

"And you'll tell them exactly what?"

"You're harassing me and my family."

Nicky shook his head. "And you, a lawyer. What are the witnesses going to say? I'm here, an old friend, pumping up your kid at a game, and you don't like it. Is that your legal standing?"

"You want to go to the mat on this?" Sam said. "You want to play with the law? I'm telling you I will go all the way. I will make sure your life is a living hell if you get anywhere near me or my family again."

"When did you change, Sammy? You used to be such a nice guy."

Sam made a fist at his side. His last fight had been in junior high school, one he lost when Bruce Weber caught him flush on the nose and blood streamed all over his shirt.

That was when he decided fist fighting was the stupidest thing human beings could do with each other.

Until now.

"You look tense, Sammy. You should try to relax."

A loud cheer went up from the stands, terminating for the moment the confrontation. Sam looked toward the field in time to see the shortstop scoop up a grounder and throw Max out at second base.

"Now that's a shame, Sammy. Maxie was a little too distracted out there."

A fresh, hot brew of anger boiled up in Sam. If this didn't stop soon—

"You know," Nicky added, "your good-looking wife seems a little distracted too."

That burst it, the last barricade of restraint. Sam's hand shot out to Nicky's neck. He pushed him hard against the chain-link fence.

"If you ever—" Sam's words stuck in his throat, stymied by the sense that he had gone too far.

But he didn't let go.

Then he felt strong hands on his shoulders, pulling him backward, and a voice shouting, "Hey man, take it easy." Sam released his grip. Two other men jumped between

Sam and Nicky.

"Don't pull that stuff here, you know?" One of men pointed at Sam. "We got kids here."

Sam looked at the stands, saw the faces looking at him. At him! While the other man was saying to Nicky, "Hey, you all right?"

"I think so," Nicky said, acting the victim, rubbing his neck.

The man who had Sam by the shoulders, a large man with an American Chopper T-shirt, said, "Why don't you take off, man?"

"Let me go." Sam felt eight years old and ashamed.

The big man gave him a little push away. "Go on, cool off."

Tense dialogue with ally

Sam has to talk to his son after the game, to explain the incident. Tension in both is enough to give the dialogue conflict.

Sam sat on Max's bed. His son's room was a mix of sports posters and black-and-white photographs. Max's hobby was photography, and he had a good eye. A sensitive eye.

Max was a sensitive soul all around. Which was what made this so hard. Sam's outburst must have really cut into Max.

"Turn around for a second," Sam said.

Sighing, Max spun around in his chair. His hair was matted and he still wore his baseball uniform. The Orioles.

Sam patted Max's knee. "You had a pretty good game today."

"Yeah."

"A nice hit."

"Uh-huh."

"You saw what happened with me and that other guy?"

Max shrugged.

"I want to explain what happened, okay?"

"You don't have to."

"No, I do. Max, this guy is someone I knew way back in college, and he's come back around to try to . . . I don't know, bother me, for some reason."

"Why?"

"I don't know. But he showed up at your game because he knew I was going to be there."

"That's creepy."

"A little, yes," Sam said, trying to keep his voice steady so it wouldn't upset Max more. "But it's nothing that can't be handled."

In the pause, Sam almost heard Max puzzling it all out in his mind.

"I'm human, Max. Maybe you figured that out by now."

Max said nothing.

Raising the Stakes

Around the mid-point of the book, Sam and Lew have a parting of the ways because the Nicky situation has Sam acting irrationally. It's affecting his work. His professional life is now on the line.

Doorway of No Return #2

A major set-back when Nicky kidnaps Heather, Sam's daughter. Now the final battle will have to be fought. Sam has a moral duty to rescue Heather.

Sam opened the phone and said, "Hi, sweetie. What's going on?"

There was no response.

"Heather?"

Laughter. Crazy laughter, like she was at a party and people were drunk and she called him and then just had people laughing all around her.

"Heather, where are you?"

"I'm safe, Daddy."

Sam's throat clamped shut. It was a man's voice, pitched high like a little girl's.

"I'm happy, too, Daddy. I got married!"

On Heather's phone. All capacity for rational thought melted in the intense heat of the unimaginable. Nicky Oberlin had his daughter.

"What, no congratulations?"

Sam could hardly speak. He felt as if Nicky was watching him right now on closed-circuit TV, enjoying the spectacle of Sam squirming, completely helpless.

"We're just so happy," Nicky said. "Can you and Linda and Max make it for Thanksgiving?"

"I want to talk to my daughter." Sam's own voice sounded tinny and distant, outside of himself.

"She can't come to the phone right now. The wedding night was really so exciting for her, she needs her rest."
"What sick thing are you talking about?"

"The wedding? That's not sick, that's a girl's happiest time! True, it was sort of my own little ceremony, it might not be entirely kosher, but boy you should have seen her, Sammy! She was beaming! And let me tell you something else, Sammy. She is a real woman. All woman, if you know what I mean."

A cold like the hands of death gripped Sam's body. "I will find you," he said. "I will find you and kill you and if you've done anything—"

"Do you hear yourself, Sammy? Is that any way for an officer of the court to talk? What a nasty man you have become! Now do you want your daughter back or not? Because, Sammy, I'm not sure this relationship is going to last."

Sam listened, numb.

"I'm going to tell you what to do to come get your daughter. See, as much as I enjoy her company, it's you I really want to see, Sammy. It's you I want to be friends with. I just had to get your attention, that's all."

Stretching the tension.

Nicky lures Sam to a remote desert house, where he has Heather. Sam falls into a pit.

His left ankle burning, Sam figured he was in pit about ten feet down.

A trap. Nicky had played him right where he wanted him to be.

Dirt and sand, and a smell like dry plants.

It was too crazy to be real. He was in a hole like an animal. This didn't happen to men like him. He was a successful lawyer. A civilized man. Trying to be a good husband and father. People like Nicky Oberlin did not exist in real life. Not in *his* real life anyway.

Heather. What was he doing to her now?

He felt around in the blackness. The pit was wide enough for him to almost stretch his arm wide. The effort Nicky must have put into this whole thing, his plan culminating with a staged setup just to get Sam in a hole.

Above him, the pit's opening was like a black disc dotted with pinprick lights. He waited for Nicky to show his face.

And waited.

Could he figure a way to climb out? He reached out and touched the wall of the trench. It was sandy, infirm. A clump fell as he attempted a grip. Trying to forge a makeshift ladder wouldn't work.

He was helpless.

And still no sounds from above ground.

"Nicky!"

No answer. Sam didn't know what he was going to say to him anyway. But if he could get him talking, that would buy time. Time for what he didn't know. It would just be more time when he wasn't hurting Heather.

"Nicky, what do you want?"

Silence.

Sam prayed as fervently as he ever had. That's all he had now.

And then heard the gunshots.

Four in rapid succession.

Then silence again, as ominous as the darkness.

"Heather!"

No answer.

I cut away to another scene. I don't want Sam out of the pit yet. In fact, I want things to get worse.

At the top of the hole, Nicky's voice. "That daughter of yours, Sam. She's a real pistol."

"What did you do to her?"

"Spunky. That's what I like about her."

"Where is she?"

"Now I have to go look for her. Like she's a dog that got out of the house."

"Leave her alone. Deal with me."

"Oh I will. I just didn't want you to be lonely while I was gone."

Sam heard a latch opening.

And then another sound. It couldn't be —

Whump.

Something hit his shoulder. Instinctively Sam jerked backward. The thing that hit him fell off and hit the ground.

And rattled.

Cut away again to another scene. We're still not finished with Sam.

Rattlesnake.

It was an unmistakable sound. In the dark he couldn't see it.

And he had nowhere to go.

The rattling got louder, faster.

Without thought, acting on pure instinct, Sam jumped and kicked out with his right foot. He wanted to get a toehold above the ground, above the snake. If he could get his foot secure, he might be able to lean across the expanse and hold himself up.

His foot went halfway into the pit's wall.

Falling back, he twisted so he could put both hands out.

And caught the other side flush. He was now hovering over the rattling sound.

But how long could he stay like this?

He calculated. If he moved upward, he risked losing the leverage he had, and falling. But if he didn't move, he'd eventually have to release.

Sam moved his right hand upward, reached out. That would be as far as he could go.

He had just one chance at this. He would have to start from the floor again. He'd have to push off with his sore left foot, dig into the dirt with his right, and give it one big push upward.

If he did this right, he might be able to get his hands over the rim of the pit. Then he might be able to pull himself out.

Might might might.

The rattling stopped. That wasn't good. Without the sound, it would be harder to calculate where to land. He could be landing on his own, certain death.

Then he heard the sound of tires on gravel. Something was going on up top.

Instinct again. He had to get out.

He dropped to the floor of the pit.

And heard the rattle rage, just before the bite. Hot needles seared his left calf.

Guess what? Cut away again. Then back.

As the bite ignited his left leg, Sam lashed out with his right. He stomped and stomped, as if trying to put out some phantom flame. Fear and rage welled up as he covered the ground where he thought the snake would be.

He felt a crunch and squish under his foot.

The head. He knew it, and kept pounding.

The rattling stopped.

Sam didn't. He kept up the jackhammering with his foot. Kept it up until he estimated the snake's head was jelly.

When he stopped, breathing hard, fire in his lungs, he realized the clock was ticking on his life.

He'd read about rattlesnakes a couple of years ago, helping Max on a school report. Some species were more dangerous than others. But what was the procedure when you got bitten?

He had no idea. He couldn't remember if it was a good thing or bad thing to try to suck out the venom. Didn't matter, because the bite was low on the calf and he couldn't get to it with his mouth.

He couldn't remember if a tourniquet was good or bad. He took off his belt, then decided against it.

Maybe . . . maybe if he could get out of the hole now, right now, he could get into the house and find a first-aid kit. The car sound had faded, indicating Nicky might not be inside.

But for how long?

Do it now. He'd climbed a rock wall at a church camp last year, on a church men's retreat. Even with a safety harness, he felt pure macho joy in it. Okay, he told himself, you are *muy macho* now. Let's see the great escape.

Sam jumped and kicked out with his right foot. As soon as he made contact, he pushed upward.

For half a second he felt poised over nothingness. He shot his arms out. His chin hit dirt, jarring his jaw.

He fell back, scraping the wall, and when he hit the bottom his left ankle was consumed by fire.

* * *

And those were my main strategies. Primarily to generate a conflict that could lead to psychological death for Sam, but also hold implications for his ability to do his job (professional) and protect his family from danger (physical).

Then I could write scenes that were organically related to

the objective, and keep the setbacks coming. All leading to a final confrontation at the end.

ABOUT THE AUTHOR

James Scott Bell is the #1 bestselling author of the classic *Plot & Structure* (Writer's Digest Books) as well as numerous thrillers, mysteries and historical novels. He is a sought after speaker at writing conferences around the world.

For a complete list of writing books by James Scott Bell, visit his website

www.jamesscottbell.com

CPSIA information can be obtained at www.ICGtesting.com
Printed in the USA
LVOW07s2020180914

404757LV00025B/733/P